Axis of Peace
Christian Faith in Times of Violence and War

Axis of Peace

Christian Faith in Times of Violence and War

S. Wesley Ariarajah

WCC Publications, Geneva

Cover design: Marie Arnaud Snakkers
Cover photo: Joel Carillet and EAPPI (Ecumenical Accompaniment
Programme in Palestine and Israel)

ISBN 2-8254-1394-1

© 2004 WCC Publications
World Council of Churches
150 route de Ferney, P.O. Box 2100
1211 Geneva 2, Switzerland
Web site: http://www.wcc-coe.org

No. 106 in the Risk Book Series

Printed in Switzerland

Table of Contents

1   1. "Do Not Weep for Me"

5   2. A Time to Reflect

16   3. The Violence of Warfare

37   4. War, Patriotism and Democracy

59   5. Religion and Violence

80   6. Violence and War in the Bible

110   7. Axis of Peace

1. "Do Not Weep for Me"

Many Christians read the Bible as part of their personal devotions. I am sure they share my experience of moments when, without ever intending to do so, one breaks off from the passage and begins to muse at length and get lost in one's own thought-world. Often it takes several minutes to bring oneself back to the passage. Such "roamings" are unplanned and unpredictable, and one is tempted to call these moments by such elevated names as "reflection", "contemplation" or "meditation"; these episodes are instances when, instead of the reader getting hold of the Bible, the Bible gets hold of the reader!

In my experience, these unplanned mental wanderings are of three kinds. The first is when one is simply awe-struck by the depth and beauty of the passage itself:

> For it is you who formed my inward parts;
> you knit me together in my mother's womb...
> My frame was not hidden from you,
> when I was being made in secret,
> intricately woven in the depths of the earth.
> Your eyes beheld my unformed substance.
>
> How weighty to me are your thoughts, O God!
> How vast is the sum of them!
> I tried to count them – they are more than the sand.
> I come to an end – I am still with you. (Ps. 139:13-18)

Then there are difficult moments when the passage does not make sense, as in Mark's account of the encounter between Jesus and the Syrophoenician woman: "Let the children be fed first, for it is not fair to take the children's food and throw it to the dogs" (Mark 7:27). I have heard many sermons trying to explain and justify the equation of the healing of a gentile with throwing children's food to the dogs. But what did Jesus really mean? One stops and becomes engrossed in thought.

The third kind of response to a passage is what I would like to stay with for a while. These sorts of passages provide challenging moments in our spiritual growth and self-understanding. Here a passage or a verse cuts deeply into one's heart and leads one to in-depth reflection on life itself.

One comes across such a passage in Luke 23.

Pilate had delivered Jesus to be crucified. Among the large crowd that followed Jesus on the way to the crucifixion were "women who were beating their breasts and wailing for him. But Jesus turned to them as said, 'Daughters of Jerusalem, do not weep for me, but weep for yourselves and your children'" (vv.27-28a).

A man who had been wrongly charged, treated unjustly, flogged, spat upon, ridiculed, and now was being led to an excruciating death, turns to the crowd weeping for him and says, "Do not weep for me, but for yourself and your children!"

One stops here. The passage takes over.

Universality of the text

In the story of the interpretation of biblical texts, this particular text has had a difficult history. It has been interpreted as an indictment of the Jewish people and the prediction of the troubled history that has marked Jewish-Christian relations in Europe. Therefore some Christians see antisemitism in the text. My own reflections, however, took me into deeper thoughts on the nature of violence in general and its impact on both the victims and the victimizers.

Is it, as many scholars suggest, Lukan sentiment that we read here? Perhaps; and yet, the text draws one into prolonged contemplation.

It is important to recognize that this sentiment, "Do not weep for me, but for yourselves and your children", could have been expressed not just in Jerusalem but in any of our major cities, not only at the time of Jesus but in our own day, and not by Jesus alone but by any person or group on whom others perpetrate violence, brutality and the shedding of blood.

A call at midnight

In 1978, I was the minister at the Moor Road Methodist Church in Colombo, Sri Lanka. Just after the general election had concluded, one of the periodic inter-ethnic riots broke out in the capital, and hooligans went around the city attacking Tamil homes and murdering innocent people. All the Tamils locked their doors and windows and moved heavy furniture against the doors to prevent them from being broken down and homes looted. Tamils' homes were filled with fear and anxiety. Adults whispered to each other as they sat in the darkness; children who sensed what was going on had to be held close and comforted.

My telephone rang near the middle of the night. On the other end was the Tamil pastor of a sister church. His house had been surrounded; some hooligans were trying to break down the front door with near success. Others had climbed the roof. He needed help immediately – "Do something! Send somebody! We are about to perish!" With the minister were his wife, his mother and three children.

Although a Tamil myself, also locked up in my house with wife and children and a friend visiting us from India, there was nothing I could have done to intervene except to ring the police over and over, and to get in touch with people whom I knew had more influence with the police. It was not easy to get through because everyone in town was ringing up the police station; it had reached the point that no one would pick up the phone at the station house. It happened that the minister's neighbours had also contacted the police earlier, and assistance had come just in time for this family. After much destruction and bloodshed the riots were quelled in the next few days.

On the following Sunday when I mounted the pulpit I saw less than half of the congregation in front of me. The other half had fled their homes into "refugee camps" (schools, temples and churches) around the city and could not yet get back to their homes. Only those who lived in the immediate vicinity of the church had dared come to worship.

I could not prepare a sermon during the previous days; my mind was not at ease and there were too many pastoral matters to attend to. I got up early that Sunday morning, sat at my desk and wondered what text I must preach on to my

Tamil congregation that had just undergone the trauma of possibly being attacked and killed. My thoughts somehow did not go in the direction of pity and compassion for those who had been or might have been victims, nor in the direction of anger and bitterness towards those who were out to perpetrate violence on innocent people. The extremists who attacked the Tamil homes represented only a small fraction of the other ethnic community, the Sinhalese, most of whom were peace-loving and compassionate. Therefore I felt sorrow and shame for my country and for all of us, in both ethnic communities, that we would allow such a thing to happen, that we would unleash violence on each other, that we who had been neighbours could become enemies overnight.

Suddenly there were no particular persons or groups for me to be angry with. How could this happen in a country where almost everyone belonged to a major religious tradition? How had we, as a people, come to believe that we would be able to resolve our differences through violent encounters? What had happened to us that we would suddenly take up the sword against our own neighbours who had lived with us in peace over centuries?!

I realized how violence diminishes us and makes us less than human. How it eats up the souls of those who perpetrate it and robs them of their humanity. How it thrives on our base instincts that we have sought so persistently to tame and overcome by building up religious systems, cultures and whole civilizations!

The text for that morning's sermon that jumped out of the Bible, as it were, was Luke 23:28: "Do not weep for me, but weep for yourselves and your children."

It dawned on me that what violence does to those who perpetrate it is even more troubling than its horrendous effects on its victims. A society that tolerates violence, a nation that is built on perpetrating violence on others, anywhere, any time, is on its way to ruin. For violence is a cancer. It eats from within.

"Weep not for me."

2. A Time to Reflect

Two days after the "shock and awe" bombing started at the beginning of the 2003 war in Iraq, one of my theological students rang up and asked to see me in my office as soon as possible. Sensing the agitation in her voice, I asked her to come as early as she wanted to. As soon as she arrived in my office, tears broke out; her hands were slightly shivering; she could hardly put words together. She wanted to be excused from attending class that day because she had not slept all night.

"What is troubling you?" I asked her gently, not wanting to pry into anything that she might not want to share. "Is there something that I or the school can do to help?" "No," she said, now collecting herself, "it's the pictures of all that bombing. They keep me awake at night. I think of all the people on whom the bombs were falling."

After some more conversation, she recovered. Even though I was ready to excuse her from class, she decided to stay on.

She had one kind of response to the bombing. Some others watched the war on television as if they were watching a war movie. I know of a few who even appeared to relish it, watching it for hours, moving from one channel to another, as if they could never have enough of it. Yet there were those, like the student who had walked into my office, who had enough imagination, sensitivity and empathy to be on the other side and to experience the horror, fear, anxiety and sheer terror of bombs falling around one and the thought of the possibility of them falling on oneself and one's family.

Those who have themselves engaged in war or had to live through wars would be aware that warfare is the most obvious, devastating and mindless form of violence. War affects whole nations, destroys peoples in large numbers, brings devastation on the environment and often renders tens of thousands of people homeless, displaced and destitute. During protracted wars people often flee their homes and countries never to return.

The human cost of war is often the least discussed. Every war leaves behind returning soldiers with deep psychological traumas; hundreds of thousands who have lost their dear ones, their livelihood and their homes; and persons who have to live with a physical or mental disability for the rest of their lives. War widows and war orphans abound in many of our nations. But most importantly, wars leave large scars in the social psyche of the peoples; the enmities and hatreds formed during wars are nursed and handed down through generations. Wars, once fought, continue in the minds and souls of peoples long after agreements to cease fire have come into effect. While firing stops on the outside, the fire of grievance and hatred lingers inwardly, ready to be stoked any time!

Human history is full of wars. In fact, All that I now recall studying in the world history courses at school and college concerned wars, empires and their rise and fall, as if it is our wars that distinguished us humans from the rest of the animal kingdom.

No country can be isolated as being more guilty of warfare than any other. A book being written over 2003-2004, however, can hardly ignore the war that has been and is so much a part of our own lives. It is said that the war in Iraq stands out from all other wars for several reasons. To begin with, it has been called the first "television war". The mass media in the USA played a significant role in preparing, justifying, promoting and portraying the war. For the first time, journalists from participating nations were "embedded" into the military and were, of course, under severe restrictions in return for being allowed to bring the war directly into our living rooms. This is also perhaps the most widely resisted war in our day. The United Nations, representing the nations of the world, and millions of peoples around the world, including millions in the USA, UK, Spain, Italy and Australia, saw no reason for this war and were actively against it. Since Iraq itself tried to avoid the war, it simply degenerated into an "invasion". Lastly, it was a one-sided war because the world's most powerful nation with its highly sophisticated armaments was attacking a nation that had little or no power to resist after having been decimated already by a previous war and twelve years of economic sanctions.

This is not a volume arguing specifically for or against the war in Iraq; it comes too late for that purpose. We are now dealing with the aftermath of the war – the daunting tasks of reconstruction, reorientation and reconciliation in the context of insurgency and resistance to "occupation". Technological precision and military might that contributed to the successful invasion are no longer of value for the task at hand. One has now to deal with *people* – their feelings, emotions, grievances, prejudices, priorities and the sectarian alliances based on religious, political and ethnic identities. People respond to events in unpredictable and unreliable ways. They change their minds; they switch sides; sometimes what we think they desperately need is not what they choose for themselves. In fact, no nation wants to be invaded, occupied or controlled by others. Difficult days are here, and more are ahead.

Some people in the United States are irritated with the people of Iraq. We "liberated" them from the dictator, and we want to install "democracy" in the country. Why would they not accept us with open arms?

The people of Iraq, however, appear to be too complex to see things in this way. People are odd. While they are happy to see a tyrant go, they seem to value honour as much as democracy, and hate occupation as much as dictatorship. These are moments when we understand Charlie Brown's friend Linus's cry of despair in the Peanuts cartoon: "I love humanity; it's people I can't stand!"

Show your hand!

For this discussion on war to be useful, I must first declare my own prejudices on the questions of war and peace. I was myself against the military action, not because I am "anti-American", "pro-Iraqi", a "bleeding-heart liberal" or anything like that. I had a very simple reason, and it was this: If there is any other way to resolve conflicts we must try our utmost to use it, because wars bring untold suffering on innocent peoples, including children who are deeply affected mentally, psychologically and often also physically for the rest of their lives. All of us are aware of the trauma of the families affected by the attack on the Twin Towers on 11 September 2001 when nearly three thousand innocent civilians lost their lives. We don't need much imagination to recognize the effects on children when some 2000 bombs fall on a city in a matter of two weeks.

The psychological scars and the hatred that result from wars – all wars, not just the one in Iraq – are too much, whether we are speaking of our own children or of others. As a father of three children myself, I dread the thought of children who lose their parents overnight and of parents who lose their children for no fault of their own. And the human damage inflicted in warfare is not "collateral"; it is the real thing.

I was also against the war on the basis of my Christian faith, but this is a contentious claim. Many Christians supported the war, and I am aware that among the leadership that decided to wage war are persons who would call themselves practising Christians. As praying and believing persons, they did not see anything wrong with waging a war even when a significant section of the international community was sure that it was not yet necessary. Leadership in the countries that supported the war claimed that they were, in fact, doing a "good" and "moral" thing by invading Iraq, because by so doing they were "liberating" the people of Iraq from an evil dictatorship and protecting the world from weapons of mass destruction.

It is important to recognize that much of the national leadership and a considerable section of Christians in the USA saw no contradiction between the Christian faith and the actions undertaken to disarm Iraq and remove its leadership. At the same time, many of the churches in the USA and the UK made clear statements of disagreement with the decision to invade. There were demonstrations for and against the war, with Christians participating on both sides.

For these reasons the war in Iraq presents us with a good example for an in-depth look at the violence of warfare. Unfortunately, it is difficult to discuss the issues and questions raised by the war in Iraq without questioning and calling to account some of the decisions and actions of the US and UK administrations that, despite much opposition, led their countries to war. My intention is not to isolate these two countries for criticism; however, they happen to be the two countries most relevant to this discussion. One could discuss many other examples of war and conflict, past and present, where leadership of different countries could equally be called into question. I ask for the understanding of those who disagree with me, or even feel offended, and hope that we may be able to consider the issues and questions that are raised by this unfortunate conflict.

Christians divided over the war

It comes as no surprise that we Christians are divided on this issue. We are also divided on many other issues – on how to read and interpret the scriptures, on matters of doctrine, on social and ethical questions and so on. Among others, two main reasons contribute to our disagreements.

First, God has created us free and intelligent beings. We have to make decisions, but they are very much influenced by how we were brought up, the kinds of influences that have affected our development, the values of the cultures that shape our lives and the nature of the information made available to us through different sources of information. It is little wonder, then, that we come to different conclusions.

Second, we are faced with difficult choices. Many issues are ambiguous. They are neither black nor white, but linger in the grey area. Often we are faced with having to choose between two options, each of them having their own "up" and "down" sides.

Take the Iraq issue, for instance. On the one hand, everyone was agreed that a brutal dictator, who had used chemical weapons in the past on his own people, was heading an oppressive regime in Iraq denying the people their freedoms. Leadership of the US and the United Kingdom (UK) administrations wrongly believed that Iraq presented an imminent threat to the USA, to the UK and to the rest of the world. Even though reliable evidence was hard to come by, many in these administrations also insisted that Iraq had connections with the events of nine-eleven. In the wake of nine-eleven, it appeared wise to eliminate such a threat.

The US administration later kept changing its reasons and goals for the war. Sometimes it was to abolish an imminent threat to the USA; sometimes it was to liberate the people of Iraq from a brutal dictatorship; sometimes it was to usher democracy into the whole of the Middle East; sometimes it was to destroy the weapons of mass destruction before they found their way into terrorist hands. On the face of it, none of them was a bad idea, and it is understandable that many Christians were in support of these goals. Who can be against democracy, liberation and national and international security?

On the other hand, many nations, and a considerable section of the people in the US, the UK and other nations, doubted the claims made by the US and UK administrations and worried about the changing goals. Some of these goals, like changing the whole Middle East, seemed overly ambitious. Other people felt that an unprovoked, pre-emptive strike by one nation on another would be against all agreed principles of international law; that it would create a precedent by which countries could attack one another on the simple perception, right or wrong, of potential danger to their own interests. Some did not think that Iraq presented any imminent danger to the USA or was in any way involved in the attacks of nine-eleven. Still others were hesitant to engage in a war against another country without the sanction of the world community, represented by the United Nations of which the US was a very important member. Others were concerned that a nation that claims to be the champion of democracy, human rights, international law, humanitarianism and so on was in danger of becoming branded as a bully and an empire-builder! They feared that the war would further alienate the Muslim world from the USA, eventually promoting more, not less, "terrorism". These reservations also made sense.

Many Christians experienced a dilemma. There appeared to be reasonable arguments on both sides. Some Christians had no hesitation in articulating their own leanings on this issue. But for many others the war presented an acute test of their faith and commitment. They asked themselves: Do we follow the leadership of the country and much of the main-stream mass media that are making an all-out effort to convince us that we must go to war immediately, without giving more time to the UN weapons inspectors? Or do we side with the many nations and sectors within our own country that see the war as premature and a clear violation of international law? Many nations were confident that, given a little more time, the weapons inspectors would be able to judge whether it was indeed necessary to employ force to disarm Iraq of any weapons of mass destruction it might have. The US administration, however, said that it had "run out of patience".

That Christians took different sides on the issue, therefore, comes as no surprise. However, the invasion of Iraq lifted up for us several questions of faith in relation to war and violence that call for more sustained study in the churches. The USA is still a very powerful country and there are today many other dictatorships, political ideologies, movements and developments with which the US disagrees. From the very beginning of civilization, nations of the world have never had a single kind of political system. There is little or no hope that all the countries would conduct their internal and external affairs to the satisfaction of all other countries or according to specific ideals held up by any other nation. Moreover, it is only a matter of time before some other countries, with different kinds of political and socio-economic life, and not particularly friendly with the USA, will also become militarily powerful.

What then?

Supposing Russia, China, Germany and France together had gone a step further in opposing the war at the security council and chose to take action to defend their economic interests in Iraq, which has the second largest oil reserves in the world. We would have had the third world war to deal with! For a variety of reasons, such a response was not prob-able this time, and the US and UK administrations were aware that this danger did not exist. But we must not forget that most wars have been fought over economic interests.

Again, supposing Iraq had in fact used on the US forces any of the chemical and biological weapons it was suspected of stockpiling in a desperate attempt to defend itself. What kind of weapons might the US have been forced to use, and what devastation would they have wrought?

Am I here painting a doomsday scenario to scare us into an anti-war position? This is not my intention. But we should not forget that we have had two world wars in the century that has just passed, with allied forces having to make enormous sacrifice of lives to defeat the Nazis. In its desperate attempt to defeat Japan, the US also dropped nuclear bombs that killed more than a million innocent people in Hiroshima and Nagasaki. World wars do not exist in our imagination; they are part of our recent history. Any country with massive military power needs only a group of misguided and self-possessed leaders in power, and irresponsible mass communication media to whip up people's natural tendency to be patriotic, and we can indeed have world wars. That's what happened in Germany in 1939.

It is for this reason that it is important for Christians, not only in the USA and the UK but in all parts of the world, whether they were for or against the war in Iraq, to look at some of the issues that have been raised for the churches in the context of the current crisis. It becomes all the more important as the US emerges as the most economically and militarily powerful nation in the current context. Power combined with excessive wealth, both in personal and national life, is a two-edged sword. People with power can do much good, provided that power is tempered by wisdom and compassion. Without power we are helpless. With power, but without wisdom, we can become reckless and dangerous.

Why a tool for reflection?

The purpose of this volume is not to engage us in a general discussion on the merits and demerits of wars or an assessment of the specific conflict related to Iraq. Much has been said and written on this issue from all sides. Rather, this book is meant as a tool for biblical and theological reflections on the issues raised by war and violence.

There are problems even in engaging in a biblical, theological discussion of these issues. Not all of us are in agreement on how to interpret the Bible. Despite some general agreements on basic doctrinal matters, my own experience shows that there are as many "theologians" as there are Christians – ask any pastor or seminary teacher!

That is the reason why this book is being written mainly as a tool for reflection. My original intention was to produce a study guide. But I found that the World Council of Churches, in relation to its Decade to Overcome Violence, already has produced a very useful study guide entitled *Why Violence? Why Not Peace?* I am also aware of other study guides on this issue in some of the churches in the USA and elsewhere.

A tool for reflection, unlike a volume on a subject, has the aim of enabling discussion. Its purpose is to animate reflection on views that we have not examined for some time, or have accepted too quickly without entering into the intricacies of the questions involved. A tool for reflection is also a means for dialogue. It has the role of helping people who come with a particular view to expand their perceptions, to enrich the views of others, to be enriched by others and to give an account of the reasons for their own position. In other words, its success depends not so much on convincing others to accept a particular view, but on its capacity to open up a question in ways that help people to make up their own minds. Whether this short volume succeeds in doing this is a matter for you to judge.

Yet a reflection tool is not necessarily neutral. Anyone who ventures into a discussion on war and violence, if he or she is true to him- or herself, would admit leaning towards one side, as I admit that I tend to do. To claim to be able to create a reflection tool that is totally neutral, on any subject, would be less than honest. I hope, however, that the analysis and questions raised in the course of these discussions will help those who disagree with me – and there will be many – to bring greater clarity to their own positions. It does not matter if we disagree to the very end. What matters in a dialogue is that we respect one another, that we truly listen to each other and that we are awakened to the depth and dimensions of the issues involved.

What are the issues raised by the current conflict?

What, then, are the matters that need some in-depth exploration? This itself is a difficult question. As one who has closely followed the debates over the war, I have identified some issues that have divided the Christians in the USA, the UK and elsewhere. What I hope to do is to give some background information on each of these issues and my own sense of what I believe is a possible Christian theological response, clearly aware that it is not the only possible response.

The issues that call for reflection, as I have followed discussions in the churches, include the following:

- Can Christians justify war? Are there "just wars"?
- What are the possible understandings of the relationship between church and state? Should Christians always support their elected governments? What does "patriotism" mean in a democratic nation?
- What is the role of religions in violence and war?
- What does the Bible say about war and violence?
- And what are possible Christian approaches to overcoming violence and war?

Others may have heard other questions, but as I now reflect back on the discussions, statements and questions that emerged during the war in Iraq and in other conflicts around the world, this cluster of issues present themselves as important matters to reflect upon. I have devoted a chapter to each of these questions.

It would, indeed, have been very difficult to discuss these issues dispassionately at the height of the Iraqi conflict. Most of us had taken sides. Some of us had our own relations or friends in the armed forces. The news media, and especially the cable TV networks, kept feeding us with information, analyses and discussions that were narrowly focused on winning our support for the war or encouraging us to resist it. But we are now at a different stage. In fact, the post-war developments and problems provide a very good backdrop to our reflections. There are new realities to contend with. The question being asked is: "We have won the war; but can we win the peace?" This is a legitimate question because it was claimed that war was necessary to bring about peace!

"For everything there is a season, and a time for every matter under heaven," says the preacher in Ecclesiastes:

> A time to be born and a time to die;
> a time to plant, and a time to pluck up what is planted;
> a time to kill, and a time to heal;
> a time to break down, and a time to build up; …
> a time to tear, and a time to sew;
> a time to keep silence, a time to speak;
> a time to love and a time to hate;
> a time for war and a time for peace. (Ecc. 3:1-3,7-8)

Now it's time to reflect.

And so we turn to the first question of "just wars". Where does the concept come from? What are its origins? What application does it have for our times?

3. The Violence of Warfare

Are there "just" wars?

"Why should we begin a discussion on violence with a consideration of wars," someone might ask. "Is it not important to speak first about violence at the personal and societal levels which might be the contributing factors to the larger issue of wars?"

I had to struggle with this question because there is indeed a case to begin with small-scale violence and to move from there to the larger and more complex issue of warfare. After some reflection, however, I decided to deal first with wars because the violence of war stands out as a separate category from all other forms of violence.

There are five reasons why the violence of war is different from other forms of violence that we shall consider in later chapters.

First, war is the most obvious form of violence that is *legitimated by the state*. Under normal circumstances the state has the duty to prevent and contain violence. If someone or a group of persons were to beat up an individual, burn down someone's property or commit murder, the state would immediately interfere and bring the person or the persons concerned to justice. In fact, all states spend an enormous amount of money to build up police forces, security systems, court systems, detention facilities and so on to contain violence. Elaborate civil and criminal laws are enacted and enforced to ensure that the society as a whole can prevent violence and dissuade individuals from acts of aggression. Wars between nations, however, are conducted by states. There are, of course, mechanisms within governing structures of all states, especially of democratic ones, to arrive at a decision to engage in warfare. But once the decision is made, there is no other authority that can prevent or control the violence brought about by war. When a state decides to go to war, the body which has the responsibility for safeguarding against violence itself engages in violence, with little or no mechanism to contain it. In other words, war is a legitimated form of violence!

Second, in the act of war, persons in the military are *forced to engage in acts of violence* in regard to which they have no personal choice. By virtue of being in the army, navy, air force or other manifestations of the military infrastructure they have to engage in violence, whether they are at the personal level convinced or not of the reasons or the justice of resorting to war. It is of course true that when persons undertake careers in the military infrastructure they are aware of the implications of their decision. And yet, war is the only form of violence in which one is forced to participate even when one may not be convinced of the need for the violence involved. This truth came home to many in the United States during the Vietnam war and finally many had to choose to go to prison, find "creative" ways to escape being drafted or simply vanish from the country in order to avoid the draft. In recent times there were at least two occasions on which we read reports of Israeli soldiers and pilots accepting prison terms rather than engaging in warfare that affected civilian populations. In other words, war is the form of violence in which one is expected to perpetuate sufferings on others as part of one's duty.

Third, a nation claims to go to war *on behalf of all its people*. Historically, we speak about war between France and England, between Germany and allied countries, between the USA and Vietnam, between India and Pakistan, as if the peoples of these nations were at war with each other or had agreed to wage war. In most countries most of the people would rather live in peace than go to war against other countries, near or far. But war is understood as conflict between nations and, what is more, there is pressure on all of us to be "patriotic" in times of war. Those who question the war during the conflict are branded as unpatriotic, friend of the enemy or disloyal to the troops fighting "on their behalf". It is of interest that one of the movements against the invasion of Iraq in the USA called itself "Not in Our Name", for wars are normally fought in our name whether we approve of them or not.

Fourth, *wars need to be won*, and such victories are celebrated by the winning nation with much fanfare. Those who fought the war bravely and inflicted many casualties on the

opposite side are considered national heroes and are deco-
rated with medals and honours. Monuments are erected to
commemorate those who have been killed in wars. Therefore, there is an urge on the part of the parties engaged in war
to inflict maximum damage and to use weapons that will
overpower the "enemy". Each side feels a profound need to
win the war.

There are of course international conventions on the conduct of war, especially on the nature of the weapons used, the
treatment of prisoners of war, the inflicting of violence on
unarmed civilians and so on. But in modern warfare, where
most of the time one unleashes violence by bombing targets
from great heights and from distant locations, much damage
is done to civilian infrastructure and to unarmed civilians.
This unjustified violence that breaks agreed conventions on
warfare is justified by the perpetrators of these acts as "collateral damage", meaning that these are part of the violence
one has to "accept" as unavoidable in war. Billions of dollars
are spent on engaging in war; then more billions are spent on
reconstruction; and many more billions again are spent to
replace military arms that have been expended. "We, the people" pay for it all, because the war was waged in our name,
and the victory is celebrated as our victory.

Lastly, war is a form of violence that is often *sanctioned
and blessed by religious traditions*. There has been a long
tradition of the religious hierarchy blessing the troops before
they go to battle, often calling upon God to bring victory to
the nation, and for the troops to prevail over the "enemy".
These days, the military chaplains and religious authorities
are more conscious of the ambiguities of war and frame
prayers and sentiments that are more nuanced. During the
invasion of Iraq, for instance, most of the mainline Christian
denominations would neither justify nor bless the war,
although they would pray for the troops who had no choice
but to go to war. But state authorities have a way of finding
religious leaders of a certain variety who are willing to give
religious legitimacy to their actions, pray for victory over the
"enemy" and bless the troops as they go to battle.

But what is more important here is not so much the actual blessing of the war but the moral and ethical justifications that are given to warfare. The invasion of Iraq was presented by the leadership in the US as a struggle between good and evil. Waging war against Iraq was painted by the leadership in the UK as a moral and ethical duty to "protect the values" of the nation. The leadership claimed to have come to a decision in an attitude of prayer and seeking God's guidance. In the USA many of the war-related events began with the whole community singing "God Bless America!"

It is not my intention here to question the sincerity of people's prayer life or their religious convictions. As I have mentioned earlier, there is much internal diversity within all religious traditions, and we do not always agree with each other on matters of theology and spiritual discernment. What is important at this point is to recognize that warfare is a form of violence that often receives religious legitimacy and justification. In fact, religions have not only blessed wars; throughout history there have been "religious wars", like the Crusades between Christians and Muslims over the sacred sites in the holy land, and many other armed conflicts conducted in the name of religion.

This sets war apart as a special form of violence that needs to be looked at closely.

Why then, we could ask, do religions, which normally reject violence, often support war that unleashes devastating violence on so many people?

Can violence and war be completely avoided?

Behind the issue of the use of violence in war lies a much more fundamental question, namely, whether violence and war can indeed be avoided altogether. There is much debate on whether as individuals and as a society we can completely avoid the use of violence. While some hold that violence of any kind should be avoided in all situations, others insist that use of violence in some circumstances is unavoidable or justified.

Let us take an example. Someone who is armed dangerously breaks into a person's house and is about to kill that person's wife and children. Would use of violence to prevent murder be justified? Or perhaps a person wielding a knife attacks one when one is walking along the road. Would violence used to save one's own life be justified?

Violence used in such cases is considered in courts of law as "self-defence" and considered legitimate in the given contexts.

This can be extended to the national level. When another country attacks a nation, it would appear that there would be no choice except to fight, and to inflict as much violence as necessary to deter invasion. This would usually be characterized as a war of self-defence. In fact, defending the nation from external attacks is deemed as one of the duties of the state, and we pay taxes to build up a military force that would be able to defend us.

The church had already come to terms with this problem in the early centuries of its life. It was part of the Roman empire that at times had to defend its territory from invaders. At other times, the Roman emperors wanted to engage in military adventure for reasons of their own. After Constantine's legalization of Christianity, the emperors put pressure on the church to justify their wars so that they could have the support of the people and of the soldiers who would lay down their lives. These were days when the church had enormous influence and authority over its faithful.

The church was faced with this dilemma: If war in some circumstances is unavoidable, what principles might be recognized to regulate the declaration of war and its conduct? . It is in this historical context that the concept of "just war" was developed in Christian thinking.

The just-war theory

It is generally believed that the early church was pacifist in its orientation. As a persecuted minority it may have had little choice in the matter. But it is also probable that Jesus' teachings and example persuaded them to espouse nonviolence as a way of life. Early historical records show that Christians refused to endorse wars or to participate in them.

There are moving stories of people who clung to nonviolence and chose martyrdom over violent resistance. Successive Roman emperors persecuted the Christians because they were suspicious of the degree of their loyalty to Rome. Such suspicions were seen to be confirmed by the refusal of Christians to join the Roman army.

The conversion of the Roman emperor Constantine to Christianity made a big difference. Christianity became the state religion of a powerful empire. The church received many benefits and concessions and temporal powers from this close association with the state. Records show, however, that even after becoming the imperial religion, Christianity by and large maintained its pacifist stance. This stance, however, was challenged especially when the stability of the Roman empire was threatened by invasion from the north. Would the church stand by and allow the empire to be decimated by an invading army? It came under much pressure to modify its position in the interest of both the state and the church.

The origins of the theory of "just war" may be traced to Clement of Alexandria (late 2nd century); it is St Augustine (4th-5th century) who developed it into a full-fledged theory. This concept that came into prominence in the Middle Ages has continued to influence the attitude to war within Western civilization. What it seeks to do is to set up at least six criteria to discern whether a particular war may be deemed by Christians to be morally justified.

The first criterion for just was is a requirement that a legitimate authority declare the war. War cannot be justified if it is undertaken by a group of people or a private militia to promote its self-interest or to settle scores with people with whom it disagrees. At the time this principle was enunciated it meant that the emperor, the king or a similar head of state must declare war. In our times it would mean that the government in power has to decide through legitimate means that the situation demands the declaration of war.

The second criterion, related to the first, is that war must be *carried out with the right intention*. This means that a nation should not resort to war with the intention of extracting vengeance, to expand its territory, to control others or for its own economic benefit. Rather, war should be undertaken in self-defence, to prevent calamities or to establish peace and justice.

The third requirement is that war be undertaken *only as the last resort*. If the purpose of war is to bring about peace, it cannot be justified unless all other avenues of resolving the issue have been exhausted. Negotiation, persuasion, dialogue and all efforts at mediation should be sought before resorting to war. In the contemporary context efforts at containment, use of economic sanctions, and so on, are used to avoid rushing to war.

These three principles deal primarily with conditions that were put in place to prevent wars. But should it eventually become necessary to wage a war, three other principles on the conduct of war were laid down in the just-war theory.

The first is the *principle of proportionality*. The temptation in war is to use excessive and overwhelming force to bring the enemy to its knees. This often results in the indiscriminate use of might, causing enormous and unwarranted destruction of innocent people as well as the infrastructure of the country. In modern warfare, sometimes whole cities are flattened and a nation's economy is brought to ruins with little hope of early recovery. The first and second world wars resulted in widespread destruction of cities and innocent civilians. In fact, unlike ancient wars, in all wars of the 20th century more civilians were killed than combatants. The wars in Afghanistan and Iraq are instances where whole nations and their economic life were totally devastated in the hope of capturing specific individuals or groups of people who were the real targets of the war. In such situations enormous social, economic, cultural and ecological devastations are brought about, sometimes without achieving the intended goals. The principle of proportionality seeks to address this problem.

The second principle on the conduct of a war is that it should have a *reasonable chance of success*. This principle, at first sight, may look rather strange because the emphasis on success might justify the use of excessive force. In reality this principle deals with the possibility of engaging in a war that has no reasonable chance of resolving the issues over which the war has to be fought. Such wars lead to numerous cycles of violence with continuous destabilization of the lives of the peoples concerned. An example helps to clarify this point. There are so many "peace initiatives" on the Middle East conflict between Israelis and Palestinians because everyone familiar with the history, demography and the respective rights of the two groups of peoples knows that the issue can never be settled by war. Sooner or later there has to be a just accommodation acceptable to both parties, and there is no alternative in the long term but for both peoples to live together in peace. In other words, there can be no military solution to the problem, and resorting to war to solve it only leads to cycles of violence and further alienation between the peoples concerned. The principle of "reasonable chance of success" seeks to dissuade parties from resorting to war over issues that cannot be resolved by warfare.

And the last principle, equally baffling at first sight, is that war should be waged with *all possible moderation*. How could one hope for moderation when the aim of war is to overcome the enemy? In fact, it is experience that dictates the principle of moderation. While a war to protect one's country may be justified, such wars should not use weapons of mass destruction such as chemical and biological weapons, nuclear bombs, carpet bombs and other arms that kill masses of people indiscriminately. Some wars have included genocides (Germany, Bosnia, Rwanda, Kampuchea, for instance) and the callous massacre of innocent civilians including women, children and the aged. The international community has established the concept of "war crimes" to bring to justice those who commit atrocities as part of warfare.

Some of the six principles above, spelt out in the context of a different age, still hold validity and have been incorporated into some of the international conventions on war in our day.

But what is important to note about the concept of a just war is that it does not seek to justify war or to encourage it. The third principle, that it should be undertaken as the last resort, shows that those who developed the theory did so as a compromise and looked upon war as something to be avoided as far as possible. In fact St. Thomas Aquinas (13th century), who worked to elaborate St Augustine's just-war theory, was pained by the way emperors abused and interpreted the theory to justify offensive wars to expand their territories. Aquinas, therefore, explicitly maintained that all wars are "sinful" and that one should first take all possible measures to prevent them.

Did the invasion of Iraq meet the principles of just war?

In contemporary history the utter devastations of the two world wars in which millions of people were killed shook the conscience of all nations. They realized that humanity should not continue to look to war as a way of settling their differences. Therefore, under the leadership of the United States, a League of Nations was established, which later was succeeded by the United Nations. The UN is a forum for dialogue among nations so that they might settle their differences through dialogue and negotiations. The UN also helped in formulating conventions agreed to by the member nations on the conduct of war, treatment of prisoners of war and refugees and so on. More importantly, the UN has worked towards the abolition of nuclear and other forms of weapons of mass destruction, anti-personnel land mines and other weaponry that kills indiscriminately. A special commission of the UN worked on general disarmament so that nations would no longer pose such a threat to one another.

Under these conventions a nation could resort to war only in self-defence. The UN, however, was aware that there might be a situation in which a militarily powerful nation might invade another nation that does not have the military capability to defend itself. Or there may be situations, as was the case in the former Yugoslavia and Rwanda, where a government or a powerful group within a nation might perpetrate genocide on a section of its own defenceless people. Such occasions may warrant military interventions to bring peace and to establish justice.

But who was entrusted to decide that a particular situation presents a global threat or internal repression to the point of requiring military intervention? Surely, it was widely argued, a country may use this provision as an excuse to invade another. In response, the UN decided that the security council, made up of all the powerful nations of the world and a few representing other nations on a rotating basis, would have the final authority to decide whether a particular situation required military intervention. The combined wisdom of a group of nations would be called for, in the form of a majority vote in the security council, for any nation or group of nations to begin a war except in self-defence. Thus, when in 1990 Iraq invaded the tiny neighbouring country of Kuwait, which could not have defended itself, the UN called upon the US and other countries to join forces to liberate Kuwait from the grip of Iraq. In other words, it is the United Nations that had the *legitimate authority* to initiate a war on Iraq, if it had turned out that it had weapons of mass destruction that posed a credible and imminent threat to the world.

Since Iraq did not invade the USA or the UK, it was important for the USA and the UK to convince the United Nations that Iraq posed an imminent threat and to get a vote of the UN security council to wage war on Iraq. Had such a vote been forthcoming, the war would have had the support of most. The USA and the UK attempted to present such evidence, but they were unable to persuade a majority of the nations that this invasion was justified. The US decision to defy the security council and to wage a war with a "coalition of the willing" was therefore described by the secretary general of the UN as both "illegitimate and illegal". He was able to say this because in this case the security council of the United Nations was the *legitimate authority* in a position to declare war on Iraq. He also expressed the fear that the US-UK action was opening up a new practice of invading a nation when it had little to do with self-defence.

The US administration, however, claimed to have its own reasons. It claimed that Iraq had been involved in the nine-eleven attack on US soil; it asserted that it had evidence of a connection between Iraq and the Al-Qaeda terror network; it alleged that it had good evidence that Iraq possessed large amounts of chemical and biological weapons and an advanced nuclear programme. In other words, Iraq posed an imminent threat to the United States and the world. The prime minister of the United Kingdom went so far as to raise the alarm that Iraq had the capacity to deliver these lethal weapons at forty-five minutes' notice.

The United Nations, however, basing its argument on reports of the UN weapons inspectors in Iraq, was convinced that there was not enough evidence for the above assertions and that one should exhaust other means of neutralizing any threat that Iraq may have been posing to its neighbours. In other words, the United Nations was convinced that the principle of *last resort* could not yet be applied to the situation in Iraq. A war, it declared, would be premature.

The third criterion of *right intention* remains one of the most debated aspects of the invasion of Iraq. Despite an intense search of the country and extended interviews with Iraqi scientists, there seems to be no evidence of stockpiles of weapons of mass destruction or of any credible programme to develop them that would have posed a serious threat to any nation. The evidence that had been produced by the US and the UK about Iraq's nuclear programme has been found to be forged and untrue. There appears to be no shred of evidence that Iraq had anything to do with nine-eleven or any links to Al-Qaeda or to other international terrorist groups. All that appears to have been unearthed is a picture of a terrible dictator who perpetrated atrocities on his people in order to remain in power. But then there are, regrettably, too many such dictators around the globe, and there is no provision in international law to remove them by the use of external force.

Internationally, few are convinced of the claim made by the US administration that the war was intended to liberate the people of Iraq and to bring about democracy in the whole of the Middle East. It is too much to ask the nations to believe that the United States was so altruistic as to want to go to such lengths and alienate its own allies and the United Nations in order to liberate the people of Iraq. And anyone who knows anything about the Middle East knows that one cannot impose democracy on the Middle East by force, especially on the part of a nation that is held in much suspicion for its unqualified support of the state of Israel. Subsequent events confirm that while Iraqis were indeed happy to see their dictator go, most of them are not thankful to have been invaded and occupied even for the purpose of enforcing a democratic government.

In the absence of any credible intentions for the war, waged at such high cost in US and coalition lives, and against the will of most nations, people are left to speculate on the *real* main intention. Is it oil? Is it more military bases in the Middle East, in search of global dominance? Is it an intention to neutralize any future threat to Israel? Is it an over-reaction to the terrorist threat? Is it just very bad intelligence? Is it a foolhardy attempt to settle scores from the earlier Gulf war?

The Iraqi invasion flounders on the principle of *right intentions*.

We need not seek answers here to the questions above. Our intention is not to fault any nation or to apportion blame but to take the most recent example of a war between nations to examine whether the principles of just war continue to serve the times in which we live. The United States, the United Kingdom, Australia and other countries are democracies with many carefully developed checks and balances concerning governance and the declaration of war. One would therefore expect that a war waged by these nations would conform to the principles of just war. The examination above shows that the claim that it was a "just war" is open to much dispute. If this be the case for a war waged by nations that are upholders of the principles of democracy, freedom, respect of international law and so on, what is to be expected of nations that hold little or no regard for these values?

Can the theory be applied in our day?

So we come to the important question of whether the just-war theory can be applied in our day. Among many competing answers to this question, I would lift up four reasons why the just-war theory is inadequate.

First, the problem with the just-war theory is that it is open to interpretation, and history shows that through the centuries successive monarchs and rulers have abused the theory to justify invasions and unjust wars. Even today the US administration and the prime minister of the United Kingdom claim for themselves the moral high ground for what they achieved in Iraq. Whatever others think about it, they claim that they acted morally, and in the case of the US even prayerfully. The problem with the just-war theory is that there is no formally authorized higher authority to judge whether the wars conducted in the name of justice are indeed just. The secretary general of the United Nations said that the invasion of Iraq was both "illegal and illegitimate", yet he had no authority or power to stop it.

The second problem with the just-war theory is that it was developed at a time when battles were fought with conventional arms. Even though the victors often committed atrocities against the victims of war, the arms used in war were themselves not powerful enough to bring about indiscriminate mass-scale destruction. Most of the battles of those days were face-to-face where armies actually engaged each other in fierce combat. Over a period of time cannons and explosive devices were developed to fight the enemy from a distance. This art has today developed to the point that one rarely sees the enemy one is supposed to be fighting. Bombs are dropped on selected targets from thousands of feet above. Satellite-guided cruise missiles seek out targets that the humans who send them never see. Weapons today, even when guided to narrowly specified targets, bring about widespread devastation of selected areas. Enormous destruction of innocent civilians and civil infrastructure are tolerated as "collateral damage". In utter desperation at not being able to halt Japanese determination in the second world war, atomic bombs were dropped on Hiroshima and Nagasaki, destroying those cities. During the invasion of Iraq there were military analysts calling for "small" nuclear bombs that would shorten the war. In any case, among the nuclear powers there are enough nuclear bombs to destroy the whole world many times over.

This means that the principle of *proportionality* and the requirement of *moderation* have become obsolete for all intents and purposes. Nations today are prepared to do whatever it takes to win wars. Any future war between two powerful nations will mean unthinkable levels of destruction.

The third problem with the just-war theory is the issue of its effectiveness in our day. It was developed at a time when the church had much influence over the population and the emperors or kings needed the support of the religious leadership in order to be able to justify the war and mobilize the population. Furthermore, at least some of the emperors believed, as did the emperor Constantine for instance, that they needed the support of God or the gods in order to mount successful campaigns. The blessing of the church and the invocation of God or the gods to give them victory were taken with some measure of seriousness.

Today we can no longer assume that those who make decisions on war are sensitive to such matters. Nations may have leaders who care little for the support of the religious communities, make decisions on war purely based on economic and political considerations and hold values that do not correspond to those behind the principles of just war. Thus, the just-war theory asks too much of the dictators and political leaders whose primary interest is to remain in power, or to be successful in the next round of elections. In our day, the narrow interests of the military-industrial complexes, the economic interests of large multinational corporations, the need to divert attention from internal problems, and so on, contributes to decisions related to war. Production, research, sale, use and refurbishing the military are the backbone of many industrial economies. Some of them even need wars from time to time to test weapons in actual battle situations. In the face of such realities the just-war theory, for all the merits it holds, fades into insignificance.

The just-war theory is primarily intended to regulate war between nations where there are clear institutions and leadership that can be called to account in regard to the declaration and conduct of wars. The reality today is that the majority of wars and conflicts are internal, between two groups within a country or between the established government of the country and a group within the nation that, sometimes with outside help, seeks to overthrow it.

Examples of internal conflicts abound: the Philippines, Indonesia, Myanmar, Sri Lanka, Nepal, Fiji, Afghanistan, the Middle East, Russia, the former Yugoslavia, Spain, Northern Ireland and numerous countries in Africa and Latin America – too many to list. In fact, more people have died in these conflicts than in the two world wars put together, and more peoples have become refugees and displaced persons today than at any other period of history. In the Middle East, for instance, third and fourth generations of Palestinians are born in refugee camps awaiting the resolution of the conflict.

The need for new approaches to resolving conflicts

The considerations above have led many people to believe that humankind *must* find other ways of resolving conflicts than resorting to warfare. The possible devastation that would be brought about by any future war has led to two kinds of responses.

The first is to advocate nonviolence and pacifism, namely, totally to reject war as a possible method of dealing with conflict. There are groups within all religious traditions, including Christianity, that advocate the pacifist position. Mennonites, Brethren and Quakers (Friends), for instance, are called "peace churches" because they completely reject the use of violence, including warfare, as a method of resolving conflicts. There are individual Christians within other church traditions who reject the use of violence. During wars they become "conscientious objectors" refusing to be drafted into the army, choosing either to accept prison terms or other forms of civil service as prescribed by law.

Within Hinduism the best-known name is Mahatma Gandhi, who insisted on dislodging the British empire from India through a nonviolent struggle. In the United States, Martin Luther King Jr insisted on struggling against race discrimination and for civil rights through nonviolent means. Buddhism and Jainism are religions founded on the principle of *ahimsa*, an approach of compassion and nonviolence towards all beings. These religions reject war, and their strict adherents would refuse to serve in the military as a matter of principle. There are significant numbers of groups within Islam and Judaism that highlight justice and peace in their respective scriptures and religious teachings and reject the use of violence and war as means to settle conflicts.

It is of interest that most people admire the positions taken by those who advocate nonviolence. Mahatma Gandhi is celebrated as the "father of the nation" and his writings on nonviolent struggle are widely read throughout the world. The United States celebrates Martin Luther King Jr Day in which much attention is given to his speeches and ministry. Peace churches are held in respect. In other words, there appears to be something deep within the human psyche that approves and admires the courage and strength to be nonviolent. And yet, those who advocate pacifism and totally nonviolent forms of struggle have always been in a minority. To many, the position, valid as it is, appears to be too idealistic and unrealistic. While they can see such a position as a personal spiritual discipline they are not convinced that nations can take the risk of total disarmament or pacifism as a national policy. This shows that there is also, deep within humankind, a fear of the "other" and the instinct to want to defend oneself and one's group, if necessary by means of force. The discussion concerning pacifism as a policy for international relations remains inconclusive.

A second modern response to the just-war theory goes entirely in the opposite direction. Advocates of this position hold that the only way to avoid war and prevent an attack on one's nation is to acquire such great military power that no one would dare to attack! The principle of "balance of power" was developed during the cold war between the Soviet Union and the Western powers, led by the United States. Both parties produced powerful nuclear weapons in large numbers and developed missiles that would deliver them on each other's cities at the proverbial touch of a button. To make the point clear, these missiles were already positioned to take off towards each other's cities within minutes once the decision was made. The fear of mutual annihilation and total devastation was believed to be the prime "deterrent" against possible attack.

This principle works on mutual fear, and to a large extent did deter direct warfare between powerful nations. Most of the wars during the cold-war period are called "proxy wars" in which the big powers challenged each other in other people's countries. Thus Vietnam and Angola, for instance, became trials of strength between the communist and capitalistic ideologies at the cost of devastation to these countries and their peoples.

The cold war ended with the collapse of the Soviet Union. However, most countries still work on the principle of developing more and more sophisticated arms as a way to prevent attack or to meet any challenge. In the United States some advocate a "nuclear umbrella" over the nation to protect it from any possible attack. Others are working to place weapons in space so that any missile directed against the country will be detected and destroyed before reaching the United States. Still others advocate the development of "small nukes", small-scale nuclear bombs that can be used even in conventional warfare with devastating impact on the enemy.

During the cold war only the major powers spent large amounts of resources in building up weapons of mass destruction. What is most worrying is that this concept of arming oneself to the teeth to prevent possible attack is catching on. Israel is the first county in the Middle East to acquire nuclear capability as protection against any possible attack. It is clear that countries like Libya, Iran, North Korea and others who also feel vulnerable have been attempting of develop nuclear weapons as the only possible way to protect themselves from the menace of other powerful nations that bully them. Many more countries are likely to go in the same direction when they have the economic means to do so.

There is, of course, a Nuclear Non-Proliferation Treaty that seeks to prevent the spread of nuclear weapons. But the very countries that try to prevent the spread of nuclear weapons refuse to give up their own weapons and have shown, as was the case in Hiroshima and Nagasaki, that they are ready to use them. The fact that powerful countries spend billions of dollars to develop more and more devastating weapons comes as no comfort to some of the smaller nations, especially when they are called "rogue nations" or part of an "axis of evil". Such designations make them feel targeted and induce them to seek nuclear capability. Nations are better prepared for war than for peace.

Is there a religious response to this reality? We shall revisit this question in our final chapter.

A new reality

The 11 September terrorist attacks in New York and Washington DC have highlighted a whole new dimension of the issues of war, violence and protection from enemy attacks. They came as one of the most devastating shocks to the nation. First there was, of course, the great tragedy of the loss of so many innocent lives. The nation was wrapped in grief. The people of New York and the whole nation united in the solidarity of agony and outrage. Almost all the nations of the world were outraged too, and there was sympathy and solidarity even from nations that normally felt distant from the US on other matters. The US administration, with its responsibility to protect its people, clearly had the right to seek out and bring to justice those who perpetrated the crime.

For our discussion, it is also important to note the many new challenges that 11 September brought to security and warfare. Four issues stand out.

First, the Twin Towers and the Pentagon were attacked as a challenge to US military and economic power not by any other country but by an invisible enemy. This is deeply troubling to a nation like the USA because all its elaborate and extremely expensive surveillance satellites, international network of spying activity on the ground and its advanced military infrastructure and nuclear preparedness are built to prevent and deter any other country or countries from attacking it. It was suddenly faced with an enemy that is not in open and direct confrontation.

Second, for the first time the US – despite its enormous military power – found itself vulnerable. It was clear that those who carried out the attack had been preparing the strike from within the country. There was no real way of knowing how many more persons were in the country and who they might be. Since those who perpetrate such attacks choose their own time and place for possible subsequent strikes, there was no way to develop a foolproof system to anticipate and prevent further events. What is more, since the US is an ethnically and religiously diverse community, there were real problems in isolating any group of persons as possible threats to national security without creating much dissension within the community.

Third, in order effectively to prevent the terrorist threat, a militarily powerful nation like the USA needed the help of many other nations. It needed the help of countries like Pakistan, Somalia and Yemen in order to be able to track down the terrorist cells. It had to coax another set of countries to trace the flow of funds to those engaged in terrorism, and yet another group to provide intelligence on the activities of suspected groups scattered around the globe. In other words, suddenly it was no longer possible for any powerful nation to protect itself by its own military power alone.

The last and most difficult task was to analyze and admit the reasons why a group of persons would go to such lengths to perpetrate violence on the United States. Should the causes that create enmity also be identified and eliminated? Those in leadership tried to give reasons: "they are jealous of our way of life", "they are against the values we stand for", "they are evil". These reasons were hardly convincing beyond US borders. For there are a number of other nations that are also "democratic", "rich" and "hold values" similar to those held by the USA. Therefore, many of the people in the USA asked, "Why? Why us? What have we done that prompted 19 young people to lay down their own lives to attack us?"

This question is, of course, the issue least discussed by the US media and politicians. It is more common for nations that have been attacked to try to take the moral high ground than to do painful soul-searching. But 11 September has brought into focus a new dimension to international conflict. Grievances are felt not only by states but also by groups of people, and some are ready to use violence to attract attention to their grievances and to seek remedy in unconventional ways. What is more troubling is that they too see their actions as "just" or "a holy war", and what happens to innocent people as "collateral damage".

There is a new dimension to international conflict, one for which we are ill prepared; one that does not fit into any of the categories of the just-war theory.

Governments of course carry the right and duty to protect their citizens from possible attacks. And yet, many look at the attack on Afghanistan as a "war of frustration" – a powerful nation's use of conventional warfare to resolve unconventional problems, resulting in the death of more innocent persons than were killed in the Twin Towers and the Pentagon, without resolving the problem of terrorism! Two wrongs do not add up to one right. And many look at the invasion of Iraq as unwise, uncalled for and devoid of any legitimacy.

Security is a legitimate concern. But how do we go about achieving it? Should citizens accept the simplistic approach of warfare as a way of resolving problems and ensuring security? Should they support any and all wars simply because their nation is waging war? When they criticize or discuss the legitimacy of wars, are they betraying the troops fighting on their behalf? Are they being unpatriotic if they oppose the war and press the government to call back the troops? These are painful issues that plague peoples in countries at war. It is to these difficult questions that we turn in our next chapter.

4. War, Patriotism and Democracy

The conflict in Iraq, its continuous television coverage, and the division within the United States over its legitimacy affected a number of people. As a professor in a university and seminary setting, I was quite taken aback by the number of students who asked for someone to talk to, and some who even needed professional counselling. I realized that the continuous and vivid coverage of the war and the endless television and radio talk-shows meant that many were dragged into virtually living the war and participating in it emotionally. Hardly any public event opened or ended without everyone singing "God Bless America". The stars and stripes were omnipresent: most homes, lamp posts in the towns, public buildings, automobiles, businesses, places of worship had flags fluttering. When I bought gas for my car at the gas station, the attendant gave me change with a little flag for my bumper or windshield. The emotional investment that most Americans had in the war was quite revealing. National patriotism and solidarity with the government and the troops were quite remarkable.

Realizing that some of the students needed pastoral assistance to take in and deal with the war and the controversy that went with it, the dean of my seminary, in consultation with the student association, organized some informal lunchhour meetings for those who wished to come together and talk about the war. Some students felt that the US had no alternative but to take on Iraq; others felt that the war was rushed and that the US should have built a truly international coalition and awaited the results of the UN weapons inspections. Different perspectives were received with mutual respect. It was good that there was a forum for people to say what they needed to say. What was important was not the positions being taken, but that there was talking and sharing.

In one such meeting there was quite a harsh criticism of the administration by some who were not only opposed to the war but engaged in organizing demonstrations against it. It was quite fascinating for me to listen to what young people were thinking on this issue. At the end of the meeting, however, I saw one of the students in tears, and her friends comforting her. I discovered later that the student simply could not live with the idea that anyone would criticize the president, the government or the United States of America. From her childhood she had been taught to be patriotic, to support what the country stood for and to admire the role the nation was playing on the world stage. She had no doubt that her country stood for freedom, democracy, human rights, free speech, free press and individual liberties, and that one should be proud and thankful as a citizen that the US was prepared to shed blood to free the people of Iraq and bring about democracy in the world. To criticize the country at this moment was unpatriotic. "Is this the support we give to our troops who are sacrificing their lives?" she asked.

Surely this was a learning experience for her. Coming from a part of the country not regularly exposed to critical thinking about her nation, she was for the first time confronting the reality that there are other Americans, equally patriotic and yet very critical of the way the nation was acting on the world stage at that moment. When I talked this over with one of my colleagues, he told me that there are three kinds of patriotism in the United States: those who love their country but can separate it from the government and the culture (or "the American way of life"); those who can separate the love for the country from the government in power, but not from the way of life; and those who make no distinction between the nation, the government and the way of life. For the third variety, the president, the country, its policies, the flag and the national anthem are all the same. One cannot let down one without letting down the others.

All this came as a big surprise to me because almost everyone I had known and dealt with in the United States, including all my colleagues and most of my students, I would say, were of the first variety. They were good and patriotic citizens but had a healthy, constructive and critical approach to the country, its policies and its culture. They treasured some of the fundamental values on which the country was founded, yet they were harshly critical of the many moments in history when the country appeared to flounder and lose track of those ideals. In fact, what they seemed to value most was that they were in a country where it was possible to be as critical as necessary of its policies and its government. This, they would argue, was the true meaning of freedom and democracy.

The relevance of the discussion

I had always valued patriotism in general, but the war in Iraq opened my eyes to the need to look again at the meaning of true patriotism in our day. However, one should immediately recognize that the concept of patriotism, and how it is expressed, differs from country to country. The appeal to patriotism has taken many forms. It was devotion to the fatherland in Nazi Germany, loyalty to the emperor in Japan, to the "crown" in colonial Britain, to the "Great Leader" in North Korea and to the ideology in many communist countries.

Nationalism and patriotism go together often, but not always. One of the problems we have in places like the former Yugoslavia, Rwanda, Sudan, and other countries is that loyalty to a group within the nation is stronger than to the nation itself. In Africa, for instance, when colonization had to be brought to an end, colonial powers drew the current boundaries of nation-states, sometimes throwing together tribal, ethnic or religious groups that did not see themselves as one people. A number of the current conflicts in Africa can be traced to this reality.

When the United States was created, the ideology that was to unite peoples who had come from many parts of Europe (and later from all parts of the world) with different cultures, languages, customs and religious traditions was presented in the image of the "melting pot". In this land, some leaders thought, the different peoples would have to be melted down into a unified nation. Now, there is much discussion about the melting-pot theory. Some challenge whether it was in fact a strongly held theory; others question the wisdom of the theory and prefer multiculturalism as a basis on which to build a society; still others, pointing to prevalent racism in society, argue that not everything was thrown into the pot!

What is important for our discussion is that the ingredient that was to hold together the new alloy was "patriotism" – the common love of and loyalty to the nation. One must admit that patriotism is strong in the United States, and it holds the nation together. However, the US has also placed enormous emphasis on democracy, free speech and public discussion of issues that affect the nation.

There is a fine balance between patriotism and democracy, especially when it comes to issues that affect the whole nation. War is one of them. Therefore, the opportunity to reflect on the meaning of patriotism in a democracy has been a very important issue in the USA. Those from other countries many not find it equally important or relevant, but I hope that the general principles discussed here will be of interest to all.

Healthy patriotism

Healthy patriotism gives to peoples of a nation a sense of belonging and unity. It helps people to rally together in times of crisis, to support and uphold one another. It gives a sense of common purpose in cherishing and defending some of the fundamental values on which the nation was built. It can inspire heroism and sacrifice in times when the nation needs to be defended. It can serve as one of the common bonds of a nation that is pluralistic in culture, ethnicity, race and religion. Above all, in many situations, appeal to patriotism may be the only force that can help mobilize the whole nation towards a common purpose.

For all these reasons, patriotism itself must be guarded from misinterpretation and abuse. The United States is one of the countries where a sense of patriotism is instilled from childhood, and most Americans are profoundly patriotic. They love their country and the values on which it has been built.

The troubling manifestations

One of the crucial issues that the war in Iraq opened up was the true meaning of patriotism. There was no doubt that the vast majority of Americans believed that it was not unpatriotic to criticize the president and the policies of the administration in normal times. But should the president and the administration be criticized at a time when the country is at war? More specifically, should the decision to go to war, the way the war is being conducted and any blunders being made be criticized when the war is in progress? Would such criticism amount to betrayal of the nation, lending aid and comfort to the enemy and letting down the troops who "have put their lives in harm's way" – as it is often described?

The answer appeared to be clear to the American cable television networks. They took no chances on the issue of patriotism. There was unqualified support for the war, and much of the reporting during the war was supportive of the government and its policies. Many of the intelligentsia of the nation and the hundreds of thousands who were demonstrating against the war, however, had a different opinion concerning what is meant by patriotism. These people were branded by some in the mass media as unpatriotic, liberal and supporters of Saddam!

The administration extended the test of its brand of patriotism to test the friendship of its traditional allies: "Those who are not with us are against us." When the French and the Germans held onto their position opposing the Iraqi invasion, the mass media and a section of the population started treating them not as traditional allies but as traditional enemies. They were described as weak, undependable, ungrateful and even archaic! People at the top levels of the administration began to talk of these countries as "Old Europe" and of the supportive countries as the Europe of the future. French wine was poured into gutters and "French fries" were renamed "freedom fries" and served with a little US flag on them.

The French themselves thought that the whole thing was rather comical. But it is important for our purposes to examine the issues involved in the response of US citizens.

Does patriotism exclude criticism?

If patriotism is about the love of one's country, is it reasonable to expect that one should uncritically support the country and especially its government when one is convinced that the country is going in the wrong direction? This question needs to be asked not only in the United States but also in all nations. Patriotism can be compared to parenting. Yes, we do love our children, but precisely because of that we need to be honest with them when we think they may be moving in the wrong direction.

This does not mean that those who disagree with the government are necessarily right. They may well be wrong, even as some children are able to educate their parents to understand that some of their fears about them are in fact unfounded. But uncritical support and blind loyalty, to one's children or to one's country, can be dangerous. Unquestioning loyalty to the emperor and his imperial designs brought ruin on Japan. Uncritical patriotism on the part of the majority of the German people helped Hitler in his designs and eventually brought havoc upon Germany.

Many people are unconscious of the reality that patriotism is one of the forces that many politicians use to manipulate the masses. Whenever some politicians say, "we are the greatest nation in the world", "we are the most powerful country in the world", "we as the leaders of the free world", "the world is looking to us for guidance", or "this is what the American people want", all my defences go up. "Tell me what you really want" has always been my response. If I simply buy that rhetoric and feel good about it, the politician is going to use me. The greatest service a citizen can do for his or her country is to be vigilant so that politicians do not drag down the country with them. At the heart of this endeavour lies the courage to differ and to speak one's mind. Those who disagree with the government are not necessarily always right; but they do us a fundamental service by keeping us vigilant.

There was a time when this all-important task in keeping a democracy alive was the responsibility of the free press and the mass media. But today much of the mass media submits in slavery to big money. Public television networks and truly independent print media are unable to compete with them on the scale needed to affect public opinion. Thus the most powerful democratic country also has the most controlled media, not by government legislation as in dictatorships, but through invisible hands that control, manipulate and impose self-censorship. "Therefore we are condemned to defend our own freedoms", said one of my students, "through organizing those who differ on the war through the Internet and actually going out into the streets in protest." Criticism and debate is at the heart of the democratic enterprise.

The same holds true in international relations. Allies are not there to give uncritical support to whatever a country does. They are committed to help one another in times of trouble. If our most trusted allies feel that we are embarking on the wrong course, it would be wiser to sit and rethink than to put pressure on them to agree, or suddenly to see them as enemies. The post-war developments in Iraq are an act-by-act playing out of the scenario that the traditionally allied countries feared would happen and about which they tried unsuccessfully to warn the US and the UK.

Why did the European allies refuse to join?

The entry into war in Iraq was one of the most heatedly contested in modern history. Several reasons contributed to the organized opposition to the war in many parts of the world. The most troubling to the United States was the refusal of some traditional allies in Europe to be part of the war effort. There were many reasons for this, but the European allies took immediate cover by pointing to the fact that the security council of the United Nations and most member states were not convinced by the evidence produced by the US and the UK that Iraq had a massive stockpile of weapons of mass destruction, and that Iraq was an imminent threat to its neighbours, and also to the UK and the USA. Even though Iraq had used chemical weapons before and had invaded its neighbour Kuwait earlier, many Europeans were convinced that the twelve years of sanctions and inspections by the UN weapons inspectors had helped to contain its ambitions. New inspections were already in place, and despite the grudging cooperation of Iraq, inspectors were asking only for more time to complete their work.

European nations were also certain through their own intelligence sources that Iraq had nothing to do with nine-eleven and Al-Qaeda, and that if Iraq had any weapons of mass destruction, they were not in large stockpiles. The US and UK administrations, however, insisted that they knew that Iraq had weapons of mass destruction and that it must immediately show its weapons and sites to the inspectors. Iraq, for its part, responded that it could show nothing because it had nothing to show. It has turned out that, this time, it was the Iraqis who were telling the truth.

There were other reasons for lack of support for the invasion. European nations have had a longer history of relating, observing and dealing with the nations in the Middle East and the Persian Gulf. They were aware of the volatile nature of countries like Iraq, and were convinced that political changes in Iraq, much needed as they were, must come from internal processes. Outside intervention, they believed, would bring social chaos and even civil war. Later events were to prove that they were right. There is no doubt that a majority of the Iraqis were happy to see the oppressive dictator go. However, with the exception of those who have achieved political and economic gains thanks to the US occupation, most Iraqis have wanted the occupation to end despite the social chaos that might ensue. Being occupied hurts the sense of honour that is central to Arabic culture.

There were other less altruistic reasons. Countries like France, Germany and Russia had enormous economic interests in Iraq. These interests were already affected by twelve years of sanctions. They feared that they would erode further with US control of the Iraqi economy and the installation of a US-appointed regime in Baghdad. Since Iraq had the second largest known oil reserves in the Middle East, everyone had an interest in who ran that country and which corporations received the oil contracts. Since US energy needs are supplied largely from the Gulf, there were deep suspicions of US intentions. Governments rarely act out of altruistic motives; countries like France, Germany and Russia saw no strategic, economic or political interests that would persuade them to join the invasion of Iraq. Countries not only have friends; they have interests.

Again, if anyone were to take steps to usher in justice, equality and democracy in the region, the USA was deemed by many Europeans to be the least qualified. Almost all Arab countries publicly or privately deplore the uncritical support successive US administrations give to the state of Israel. They do not believe that the US, because of internal pressures and strategic interests, can ever deal even-handedly with the Middle East conflict. The intensifying conflict in the Middle East has been used by Arab media and leadership at popular levels to present the US as the enemy. The fanning of hatred has been so successful that at least twenty young men were convinced to give their lives flying planes into US targets.

Most importantly, the US and UK administrations' reasons for having to invade Iraq appeared to Europeans very unconvincing. When the threat, in the opinion of those who knew the reality, was not real, why would these nations want to invest so much of their resources and people's lives to go to war? These considerations led to the belief that the invasion of Iraq was part of a grand strategy on the part of the US to build a New American Empire in the 21st century. These suspicions were being fed by ideologues close to the US administration who spoke of a "second American century", of America's "manifest destiny" to be the leader of the free world and the "exceptionalism" promoted by the US administration. The administration had already been alienating other nations by withdrawing from agreed international treaties, refusing to sign new treaties and acting unilaterally on international and trade issues.

Many nations, rightly or wrongly, saw the intended invasion of Iraq as part of a grand strategy. These fears were confirmed by the fact that in turning its interest on Iraq, the US had begun to lose interest in bringing about the democratic transformation of Afghanistan, which it had said was its aim. Once it had installed a US-dependent regime in Kabul, and had established strong and permanent military facilities in the country, it turned its attention to Iraq. The interest in Afghanistan, it was assumed, simply had involved capturing Bin Laden.

There was more. Even though the American armed forces made enormous sacrifices to free Europe during the second world war, European populations had taken much of the brunt of devastation that the war entailed. The memories of the destruction brought by war are still alive in Europe. Therefore European populations generally have been opposed to nations resorting to war unless there were unavoidable reasons for doing so. Even though they are real-istic and continue to build their defence capabilities, psycho-logically there is little interest in Europe in a display of power and might through building grand military arsenals and showing the nations' prowess and the latest military capabilities in actual war situations.

Again, none of these nations appears to have the feeling that is so prevalent in US thinking, that some "other" nations are building up massive arms and are waiting in the wings to attack one day. This fear leads the US to continue to spend massive amounts of money on such ambitious programmes as the nuclear umbrella, space-based weapons and further refining the capabilities of missiles that may be launched at specific targets from air, sea and land. Europeans, for their part, appear to believe that wars must be prevented at all cost, and the best way to do it is to forge closer economic links with other nations, through trade diplomacy seldom dis-cussed in public. The cultural gaps between the continental Europeans and the US in this regard are quite remarkable. The US's eagerness to get to war in Iraq was seen in Euro-pean capitals, rightly or wrongly, as an over-reaction to the tragedy of nine-eleven, US ambition to exert itself as *the* world power, an attempt to control the Iraqi oil reserves or simply the exploitation of American patriotism for political ends. None of this kind of thinking would make sense in the USA. Most of the people in the USA would vouch for the morality and sincerity of their nation.

Over the past several decades, European societies have been growing into multi-ethnic, multicultural and multi-religious societies through immigrants, refugees and asylum-seekers from the Middle East, Eastern Europe, North Africa and several other parts of the world. One of the results has been the significant growth of Islamic populations in Western Europe. Today there are more Muslims in France than there are Protestant Christians. Unlike the American vision of the melting pot, Europeans tend to see multiculturalism as the ideal, where each of the communities are encouraged to be who they are within a formally and informally agreed principle of mutual respect and loyalty to the nation. Xenophobia, neo-Nazism and religious militancy are always lurking nearby, so European governments are particularly keen not to engage in acts that could provoke internal turmoil. The last thing they needed in 2003 was an unprovoked war against an Islamic nation. It is this sentiment that expressed itself in the anti-war stand of the people of Spain, who were already suffering from internal struggle and violence over the demand for the independence of the Basque region. The Madrid train bombings of March 2004 confirmed their fears, and they decided to punish the administration that dragged them into a war in elections that followed the bombings.

Social cohesion can never be taken for granted; it must not only be carefully built but also protected and nurtured. This is true not only for Europe but for all countries. By resorting to war in Iraq against the will of the United Nations, the US was squandering the good will and the solidarity it had engendered among all nations after nine-eleven, and members of the coalition of nations it had built to take on Afghanistan for harbouring Al-Qaeda.

The US-based cable TV channels and most hosts of radio talk-shows appear to have no awareness of these realities. At least one of the major cable TV channels began to feed anti-

European sentiments with a vengeance. As for the administration, for whatever the reason, it had already made up its mind and was too bent on having its way to listen to any reasoning from its friends and allies.

The right kind of patriotism was much needed at this time, but it was in short supply.

Should the war be discussed while it is in progress?

The most difficult question in this area is, once the war has been declared and is in progress, whether the act of war itself and its conduct should be subjects of public debate and discussion. Criticism of the administration over the declaration or the conduct of the war is considered by some as unpatriotic acts that aid the enemy and weaken the country. The more common argument is that such criticism amounts to lack of solidarity with the troops who "put their lives in harm's way" for the sake of the nation. A sensitive issue here also relates to the members of the families of persons on the battlefield. It would be difficult for members of the families to feel that their husbands, wives, sons, daughters, brothers, sisters or parents might be killed in a war that is not supported by the nation.

Those who support the war cite these reasons to try to silence any meaningful debate of a war in progress. Much pressure is employed to gain support for the leadership in decisions they make and to overlook what others may consider to be decisions that would be detrimental to the national well-being.

This is a difficult issue, and these arguments are used effectively to quell much public discussion of a war in progress. No person wants to be called "unpatriotic" or the "friend of the enemy" at a time the nation is at war, and certainly no one wants to be branded as "betraying" the troops or being "insensitive" to the feelings of family members.

At first sight, the arguments against public debate do appear to be solid. Difficult, sensitive and complex as it is, this issue needs to be looked at more closely.

There are some assumptions in these arguments that need closer examination.

Are all wars in defence of the nation?

Most people assume that if their country goes to war it does so on their behalf, mainly to protect them from enemies, and therefore the war effort should receive their full backing. People who have studied past and recent wars, however, point out that warfare is a much more complex affair. In ancient times small tribes fought wars against neighbouring tribes to control or defend their land, cattle, water-holes and other possessions. Most of the male members of the tribe would fight and the battles were limited in scope. The damage done was also limited because of the kinds of weapons that were in use.

Gradually as kingdoms emerged, kings began to set aside groups of men to specialize in the art of warfare, both for their defence and for offensive purposes, leading to the emergence of what we now know as the "army". Over a period of time the size of armies grew, and weapons of war became increasingly sophisticated. The capacity to fight from a distance with guns and cannons encouraged kings, emperors and colonial powers to embark on large-scale warfare to expand their territories, to control trade routes and to amass wealth. Many of the wars were for economic considerations. Scarcity or the attempt to control important resources such as fertile lands, mineral deposits, oil and so on can lead to wars between states. Some predict that, unless we invent affordable ways of converting sea water into fresh water, wars of the next centuries, as population grows, may be over the control of fresh-water resources. During the cold-war era ideology played an important role in the war between states.

Many wars at local levels arise as conflicts between ethnic, religious or national groups, especially when a majority group attempts to monopolize power, or a minority group that has captured power attempts to keep it through brutal force.

In our own day what has become prominent in the discussion on war is the role of special-interest groups. In most countries it is well known that special-interest groups attempt to lobby governments, contributing large sums of money during elections to ensure that those elected leaders legislate in ways favourable to them, and even attempting to take control of the government to protect and further their interests.

While people go about their daily life, and are satisfied if the conditions of their lives are reasonable, these groups can manipulate the governments or collaborate with them to further their interests, even by resorting to war. The finger is pointed in most of the Western industrialized countries at the "military-industrial complex". Most of the citizens are not conscious that the military is a war machine as well as a huge economic industry. Each year several hundreds of billions of tax dollars are paid to maintain the military, to improve its capabilities, to do advanced research and to develop and test sophisticated weapons. It includes the budgets, not only of the military machinery and of scientists and researchers, but also the cost of contracts worth billions, paid out to large corporations, to build new weapons.

A major war, therefore, has massive economic consequences. On the one hand there is large-scale destruction; on the other, there are lucrative contracts to rebuild what has been destroyed, to refurbish the army, to improve the weapons used or tested in the war, to do further research and to build new weapons. War is perhaps the most profitable and employment-creating industry of our day in the Western world. In some Western countries, the military-industrial complex has become the biggest employer. Today, many studies have shown that it is possible to diversify the economy and maintain high levels of employment without having to depend on the military-industrial complex. But that redevelopment needs enormous courage to implement and the willingness to take on powerful lobbies and calculated risks. This has been made almost impossible by a donations-driven electoral process in which candidates need to raise millions of dollars to be elected to leadership. In the meantime, warfare remains the most profitable business.

Economic interest related to war is also prominent in the poorer nations of the South. Most of the dictators, and people in leadership in government, spend much of the nations' scarce resources to buy weapons to ensure that they stay in power. While doing so they put away millions of dollars they receive as "commissions", "kick-backs" or bribes in foreign banks in their names or in numbered accounts. Almost every dictator deposed from power in third-world countries and even some elected heads of states have been found to have put away millions in their names as part of procuring arms to "maintain peace" in their countries.

To average citizens like you and me, such accusations on the part of those who analyze and study warfare may appear far-fetched or ethnically biased. We want to believe that our government would never do such a thing! Military budgets never attract our attention because we feel that we need to keep armed forces in place for our own security. We seldom make the connection between warfare and profits running in the millions.

It is significant that many countries of the South have called the war in Iraq an "oil war", because they suspect that with the increasing demand for petroleum, a non-renewable resource, the big companies that deal in oil would like to control nations that sit on substantial oil deposits. We are aware that the countries that invaded Iraq have rejected this accusation. It is certainly not uncommon for people to develop conspiracy theories over actions that may well have been taken with appropriate motives. In fact, the intention of this discussion is not to suggest or to prove that the war in Iraq was motivated by special interests of the military-industrial complex or by the oil barons. That investigation needs to be left to the experts.

Rather, this whole discussion shows that war, the motives of war and its conduct need to be discussed in a democratic nation, since not all wars are intended to defend the nation.

The simple fact that a war has begun is not sufficient reason to stop citizens' discussion, unless of course it is a war to repel a direct attack of an invading army.

There are many other reasons why a war, any war, must become a subject of discussion and debate in the countries engaged in war. The war may have been ill prepared; it may have no chance of success despite sacrificing the lives of people; it may be conducted in ways that defy international humanitarian conventions; it may end up costing amounts that a country will never be able to afford; after the beginning of the war, alternative ways of resolving the conflict may have been discovered. In other words, warfare is a tenuous business; it is a risk that a nation takes to solve a problem in a particular way. As it progresses, both the leaders and the people whose sons and daughters are on the battlefield need to consider the nature of its progress, the possibility of it achieving its goals and the advisability of pursuing it to the bitter end. This is what eventually happened in Vietnam. But by the time people awoke from their blind patriotism, an unacceptable number of lives had been lost on both sides in a war that had no chance of ending in anything other than stalemate or defeat.

It has been said that the first casualty in a war is truth. Iraq's minister of the interior was telling the people of Iraq that its brave armed forces were defeating the Americans and holding them at bay, and that Baghdad would be defended to the very end. But the people of Baghdad had only to look out of their windows to see US forces rolling into Baghdad and taking control of the centre of the city with hardly any resistance!

"Comic Ali", as the interior minister came to be known, is an extreme example. But it is known that political leaders and commanders of the armed forces frequently fail to tell us the truth during war. They need to put on a brave face, claim that everything is going well, assure the people that the sacrifices being made are worth it and that victory is at hand. In this way the necessary debate is postponed, sometimes until it is too late.

It is in everyone's interest that in a democratic country debates are held on all matters, including warfare. This also holds during the conduct of war, for the reasons given above. A war indeed may be started for the wrong reasons, conducted in unacceptable ways and may outlive its purpose. How would we know, if we were not allowed to talk about it?

Do we betray the troops when we debate a war in progress?

The most effective way criticism of wars is contained is by arguing that such criticism affects the morale of the troops in the battlefield. "When people are putting their lives on the line," it is argued, "the last thing they want to hear is a report of debates back home on the legitimacy of the exercise. What they need is support and solidarity." Normally this argument is further strengthened by appeal to the feelings of the next of kin of the troops. "Are we being sensitive to the feelings of the relatives of our troops?" one is asked, "Would you be saying this if your own son or daughter were at the front?"

These are good questions and we need to take them seriously. During the "prayers for the people" in the chapel services at the seminary where I teach, individuals would name persons who are their sons, daughters, brothers or friends who had been sent to Iraq. Sometimes this was done with much emotion. Prayers were said regularly for those men and women who had been sent to the front.

And yet, we need to examine the *assumptions* made by those who say that to discuss the pros and cons of war would be to betray our troops.

First, we need to recognize that serving in the army is a professional activity. Except in situations where one's own country is under direct attack and men and women brace themselves to defend it, if necessary with their own lives, much of the rest of warfare is carried out by professionals. In most circumstances men and women do not go to war; they are *sent*. And, having chosen the military as their profession, they must follow the disciplines involved, lest they be court-marshalled; in fact, they have no choice but to go to war when they are sent by the higher-ups.

A soldier sent to the battlefield may share the passion, ideology and rationale behind the war that is being fought. On the other hand he or she may be in complete disagreement with the purpose, the goals and the need for the war itself. He or she may even think that it is not a worthy cause for which to lay down one's life. But these convictions have little to do with the need to fight if one is sent into battle. History is full of events when mad, ambitious or crooked emperors and rulers have sacrificed the lives of millions to achieve their unworthy ambitions, to satisfy their egos or simply to display their power and might and to expand their territory. In such situations the troops do not sacrifice their lives; misguided rulers sacrifice them at the altar of their ambitions.

Unfortunately, rules of engagement prevent soldiers in the field from openly and honestly speaking about their own assessment of the war or of their involvement in it. From time to time we come to know about those who refuse to go to war on the basis of their conscience, and of those in battle who would rather get back to the loved ones they left behind. These instances are rare because soldiers are, in the interest of military discipline, prevented from expressing their real feelings and from refusing to go to war when ordered.

One supposes that such discipline is necessary in military service. There needs to be a line of command, and if each soldier were given a free choice in the battlefield wars could not be conducted. This is understood by those who enlist in the military as a career. In most situations they continue to understand and live by that discipline, sometimes even sacrificing their lives for causes they do not believe in.

All this means that the only voice the troops have in these matters is provided by people back at home. They have to depend on the people to prevent them from being forced into causes that are not worthy, from being sacrificed in battles that cannot be won and from being used in causes that are illegal or illegitimate.

Troops have no say in the war; it is only the people outside the armed forces who have a say. It is such people's duty to ensure the safety of the troops by challenging wars that put soldiers in harm's way for questionable reasons. In other words, if we think deeply enough, we owe it to our troops to see that debate on war is kept alive and leaders are kept accountable. This is the minimum that those who do not actually go to the battlefield can do for the troops.

On many occasions those who appeal for "loyalty and solidarity" with the troops do so in order to prevent legitimate criticism of a war. They do so not because they are in solidarity with the troops, but because they are keen to promote their own designs. Their appeal to patriotism on these occasions is phony; true patriotism is to demand the right to hold those who send our troops to war answerable for their actions.

Democracy and patriotism

Ultimately the demand for patriotism during war and indeed at all times has to be understood in the context of the meaning of living in a democratic society. The much-quoted Lincolnian saying on democracy is that it is "of the people, by the people and for the people". This has of course been expanded and expounded in many ways in political science circles. But the most important dimension of the saying is that the government of a country is chosen by the people and is accountable to the people. We hold elections to choose the persons who will play the key roles in governing the nation. We do this once every four or five years, as the constitutions of specific countries require. Once a government is elected on the basis of the policies and plans it advocates, we tend to give leaders considerable space to act, recognizing that there needs to be trust between those elected and those who elected them for the ongoing life of the country. But a government is never above its people, and it has to take account of the people's opinions. It was surprising that the governments of the United Kingdom and Spain, for instance, on the issue of going to war in Iraq, would make decisions that defied the vast majority of their people's opinion.

But even when the people support the war (on the basis of information made available to them), as in the case of the USA, they have the duty to hold the government accountable for activities undertaken in their name. In a democratic society this takes place in discussions, debates, encountering opposing views and convincing one another. Taking a country to war and maintaining a long drawn-out conflict is a serious national question. Billions in taxpayer's money are allocated; the nation's standing in the international community is at stake; lives of troops and innocent civilians are involved. These realities demand that there be a continuous, democratic debate on the issue.

Citizens' participation in a democratic nation does not end with voting. In fact, electing a government is only the beginning. Continuous interest, involvement, support, criticism, protest and debate are at the heart of a democratic society. This is also a key to the meaning of true patriotism.

Religion and patriotism

Many years back, when I first came to the United States as a visitor and attended my first worship service in a church, I was struck by the fact that on one side of the altar stood what appeared to be the flag of the church or the denomination, and on the other the stars and stripes. The symbolism was clear. People of the church are for "God and country".

At first sight there seems to be nothing wrong with this. It is quite possible for a person to be a faithful Christian and a loyal citizen and to hold the two together. In many religions, like early Judaism and Islam, the religious laws or teaching include the way political life should be organized. Several countries have a theocratic model of governance, which means that the political life is organized by laws that are religious or deemed to have been revealed by God. Some states today declare themselves Islamic states. In Christian history church and state have been very close to each other; even today there are state churches in some parts of Europe as relics of their history. There have been Buddhist and

Hindu rulers who sought to rule the country according to the respective *dharmas* (teachings).

In our day, several countries like India, France and the United States have made a clear separation between religion and state. In a country like India this is done in view of the religious plurality of the nation. The state remains "secular" in the sense that its policies are not developed in respect to any one religious tradition or its teachings. In the West the separation was introduced partly because of corruption that had entered the churches when they had acquired temporal powers. The tensions between the popes and the emperors and locally between the bishops and the feudal lords fill the pages of European history.

The constitution of the United States requires a strict formal separation between church and state, or religion and state. In theory, this means that while political leaders can be deeply religious, as many have been and are, they are not to make their own religious convictions the basis of the policies of the state. On the part of religions, while the faithful and the religious communities are free to participate fully in the political processes of the nation, religious systems as such have no official role in the administration of the political life of the nation.

Why, then, is the flag hoisted next to the altar?

The answer lies in the mythology that was part of the founding of the United States. To the early settlers, fleeing to the New World from turmoil in Europe, the land that was to emerge as the United States was the "promised land", and the new people, the New Israel. As the New Israel, it stood in a special relationship with God. Its "manifest destiny" is to be a light to the nations. God has willed it. Therefore, despite the legal separation between religion and state, all the currency carries the national sentiment: "In God we trust." And "God Bless America" is sung both in church (on national days) and the national anthem, "The Star-Spangled Banner", is sung in the baseball stadium before the game begins. Those who have no religious beliefs, and are ardent supporters of the separation between church and state, will sing these songs with gusto, even with tears rolling down their cheeks! The church-state relationship in the USA, at the legal level on the one hand, and at cultural levels on the other, is quite fascinating but is beyond the scope of this discussion.

What is important is that in many countries patriotism and religious beliefs get mixed up. While this may not present a difficult problem in day-to-day living, it becomes a big issue during a war. Should the church throw itself behind the nation in times of war? Or should it keep a prophetic distance from the state and engage in criticism when the state appears to be moving in a wrong direction? Christians are divided over this, too, and the Bible can be quoted on both sides. On the one hand, the Bible says that all secular authority is given to us by God, and on the other, perhaps no other religion's scripture has such devastating and fearless criticism of the rulers by prophets when they saw the nation being taken in the wrong direction.

The openly and implicitly religious language that has been used to justify and rally support for the Iraqi war is one of the important issues that needs to be discussed. What is the relationship between faith in God and support of the state? What is the relationship between patriotism and belief? These are among important issues that have been raised by the war in Iraq and should be followed up in the religious communities.

We should leave Iraq and the specific discussion of war and patriotism at this point. As was said earlier, war is the most obvious and devastating form of violence. But a discussion on overcoming violence needs to be part of a broader conversation on the many ways in which violence manifests itself. We begin with a consideration of the relationship between religion and violence.

5. Religion and Violence

About two years back my former colleague in the Office of Inter-religious Relations at the World Council of Churches, Hans Ucko, called me over to talk about organizing an interfaith encounter on religion and violence.

Very soon we discovered that this would be a difficult meeting to put together, because persons representing each of the religious traditions would quote their scriptures to show that their religion stood for peace, love and harmony. No religious tradition sees itself as one that supports, condones or is the source of violence and conflict. Therefore, we decided that we needed to think hard on how we would formulate the invitation. We needed first to acknowledge that all our religions are for peace, harmony and unity. And then we must put to ourselves the question, "Why and how, then, are all our religious traditions so closely associated with violence?" This approach was helpful and we had a fruitful encounter.

In his editorial in *The Ecumenical Review* of April 2003 that carried the presentations from this meeting, Ucko framed the issue that was placed before the group: "It is true that Islam is literally a religion of peace. It is true that *Om shanthi, shanthi* (peace) is the emphatic Vedic blessing. It is true that Jesus greeted people with the gift of peace, 'Peace be upon you.' It is true that there is an absolute emphasis on compassion and *ahimsa* in Buddhism. It is true that Judaism has given the world the word and concept *shalom.*"

Why then, the question followed, are religions so intimately involved in situations of violent conflict? Is there a problem in the way religions define themselves? Is a tendency towards violence inherent in the way religions look at each other? Or are religions so closely aligned to the political and social realities as to be used and abused by forces that care little or nothing for the ideals that religious traditions hold?

It is all too common for religious leaders to place the blame on social and political forces for the association between religion and violence. However, many recent writings have begun to challenge this easy assumption. In his volume *Terror in the Mind of God: The Global Rise of Reli-*

gious Violence,[1] Mark Juergensmeyer studies several concrete violent situations and specific events to show that religious beliefs and convictions do in fact play a pivotal role in inspiring and justifying some forms of violence. Increasing numbers of analysts trace violence to the very heart of the way religions have been conceived, taught and practised. There are even those who believe that religions are the fundamental problem and that a world without religions would be a more peaceful place in which to live.

There are, of course, others who dismiss this claim as cynical and look at religion as the only hope for peace and harmony left in a world that is increasingly secular, materialist and intolerably violent. They would argue that, despite all the compromises in the past and the present, religions still hold the seeds of hope for the renewal and reawakening of the spiritual dimensions of human life.

The considerations above show that "religion and violence" is a complex issue. And the complexity has to do, for the most part, with the ambiguities that surround both the words "religion" and "violence". The word "religion" connotes different meanings to different people. Even the use of the rigid and static word "religions" to characterize the many ways of life, spiritual orientations, practices and profound insights into the nature of existence has been criticized. Wilfred Cantwell Smith, one of the pioneers in this field, has pointed out that the word "religions" emerged out of the Enlightenment culture that needed to define clearly and demarcate boundaries so that the phenomenon could be critiqued and studied. The Hindus, for instance, never developed "Hinduism" as a "religion". In fact, there is no entity that has called itself "Hinduism". It is a name that was imposed on the many spiritual insights, paths, teachings, philosophical explorations and spiritual practices that were part of the life, culture and spirituality of the peoples who lived in the Indian landmass over some three thousand years.

---

[1] Cf. Mark Juergensmeyer, *Terror in the Mind of God: The Global Rise of Religious Violence*, Los Angeles, Univ. of California Press, 2000.

Similarly, some of the Jewish scholars say that "Judaism" is a word imposed on the Jewish way of life by Christian scholars of the early centuries after the time of Jesus.

Moreover, no particular "religion" is a static reality. Since it is a lived reality, it is always in a process of evolution and manifests itself in many ways. There are many forms of Christianity, many branches of Buddhism and many streams of Islam, and none of them have remained the same through the centuries. Therefore Smith prefers the use of the phrase "cumulative traditions" or "religious traditions" rather than "religions" to denote the reality we are speaking about, and separate it from other dimensions like "faith" and "belief". Much can be said here, and I find Smith's argument quite persuasive. But I doubt that today we can run away from the conventional use of the word "religions" to denote groups of persons who have, however loosely, organized themselves as part of a symbol system. Much against my own instincts, therefore, I will use the word "religions" in this discussion so that we may hear of the conversation on "religion and violence".

In order to get to the issue of violence one must first highlight some dimensions of what has been understood as "religion" that contributes to the complexity of our contemporary discussion.

Religion as a social phenomenon

Some years back, while I was still working on interfaith issues in the World Council of Churches, I was asked to give a talk to a visiting group of leaders from the United Methodist Church in the USA. The group was on its way to Russia for a dialogue with the leadership of the Russian Orthodox Church. The communist system that had systematically taught atheism and communism to successive younger generations had collapsed; the former Soviet Union was no more. This fall of communism, in the Methodist view, provided a golden opportunity for evangelism. Revival of the Methodist tradition in Russia and a concerted programme of teaching and preaching the gospel would help the emerging new Russian society to recover its Christian moorings that had been so badly damaged under communist rule.

On the face of it this was a noble effort. A Protestant might well think the Russian Orthodox Church should be happy at any evangelistic effort that would "re-Christianize" the Russian peoples. But the Russian church did not think so. When speaking with leaders of the Russian Orthodox Church, one comes to the realization that we are here dealing with two different world-views about religion and its place in society. United Methodists were looking at religion as a matter of free choice. For them, one normally is born into the denomination of one's parents, but being a Methodist, a Baptist, a Presbyterian, a Pentecostal or for that matter part of any other of the major religious traditions of the world, in the last analysis, has to be a matter of personal choice. Religious freedom, in this view, demands that one have the choice of the religion and the denomination to which one belongs.

In Russian Orthodox thinking there is an inalienable link between the nation, its people, its culture and its religion. If one were born in Russia, spoke Russian and was of the Russian culture, it was thought natural and normal that one would also be Russian Orthodox. In fact, in most countries where the Orthodox church is the predominant religious tradition, the church has always looked upon itself as the custodian of the well-being of the culture, language and spirituality of the whole nation.

In the Methodist point of view, if the Russians are truly ecumenical, they should allow for other denominations to engage in evangelism and church planting. In the Russian view, if the Methodists are genuinely ecumenical, the only thing they should do is to help and strengthen the Russian Orthodox Church to re-establish itself as the spiritual guardian of the people of Russia!

It is not my intention here to examine the merits and demerits of these two positions, but to indicate that most religious traditions are also social phenomena. Religion expresses itself not only as a spiritual path but also as the force that gives identity, cohesion, profile and sense of belonging to a community. In fact, most of the religious communities, especially those with a monotheistic orientation, have a strong sense of group identity. The Jewish tradition puts enormous emphasis on its peoplehood; the Christians take pride in the church universal; the Muslims tell of the Islamic *umma* and so on. It is little wonder that religion becomes part and parcel of the vicissitudes that befall these communities. When a community is in conflict, religion invariably becomes an element in the discord. Three examples might be given to illustrate this reality.

Religion, peoplehood and the land

It is part of the self-understanding, probably of the majority of the Jewish people, that God chose them, gave them the Torah and entered into a covenant relationship with them to live out God's justice and righteousness among the nations. Practising justice and righteousness in concrete terms requires a land to live on. It was also believed and affirmed in Hebrew scriptures that God promised them the land of the Canaanites, which constitutes much of the land inhabited by the Israelis and Palestinians in our day.

In the contemporary scene there is a diversity of opinion among the Jews themselves on the exact nature of this "promise". Some would say that the Torah has to be practised in one's heart and in one's home, which symbolically is the "land" where God's righteousness has to be lived out. Others would say that the land does not constitute a particular piece of land in the Middle East but any land on which one happens to live. The land on which one lives becomes the "holy land" when it is a place where God's righteousness is lived out. These interpreters would distance themselves from the events in the Middle East and deplore the way the community is being drawn into a cycle of violence.

However, there is also a considerable section of the Jewish people who hold that God specifically promised the area where Israelis and Palestinians live today to the Jewish people, with Jerusalem as their capital. Even though the creation of the modern state of Israel was precipitated by rampant

European antisemitism and the Nazi holocaust, political aspirations became mixed, for sections of the Jewish community have been motivated by religious zeal that began to see the settling of the whole of the land and recovery of Jerusalem as its capital as a religious obligation.

The problems inherent in this religious self-understanding are obvious. It is very difficult for outsiders, who are not part of a religious community and its cherished beliefs, to challenge its religious self-understanding. At the same time there are also no objective criteria to judge whether God in fact promised a piece of land which was already occupied to another group of people who had to take it, according to the biblical narratives, by use of enormous force.

Some Christians, who read the Bible quite literally, believe that this latter understanding must be true, just because the "Bible tells us so". Who are we to challenge God's promises and actions so clearly set out in the Bible? But those who study the Bible with a critical eye would claim that Hebrew writers who wanted to give religious sanction and legitimacy to the occupation of the land wrote the "historical" books of the Bible to place the burden of their ancestor's own actions on God. The focus of discussion often shifts at this point to questions about the nature of the Bible and the legitimacy of interpretations.

The problem is that history is never neutral; it is always told from a particular standpoint. This came home to me when I heard that the Native Americans describe their own history as "Canaanite history" – a history from the perspective of those who were conquered and occupied. No amount of biblical or theological explanations would convince people who are forcefully displaced from their homes and villages that it was God who willed it. And one of the major problems in the Middle East is that different peoples were thrown out of the land at different periods of history, and all parties look upon themselves as the victims.

What is important for our own purposes here is to note how religion can and does become so deeply intertwined with people's socio-political self-understanding and thus becomes hopelessly embroiled in violence and counter-violence as seen today in the Middle East.

The battle over Ayodhya

A similar problem has been in the making in India with the arrival of the Hindu nationalist ideology known as *hinduttva,* the "Hinduness" of India. Briefly, this ideology sees Hinduism as the religion of Mother India, which constitutes the whole of the *punyabumi* (the holy or sacred land), the Indian sub-continent. The problem, of course, is that India is already a multi-religious country with a considerable population of Muslims, Sikhs, Jains, Buddhists, Christians, Zoroastrians and so on. Moreover, what is considered the Motherland has already been divided into India, Pakistan and Bangladesh, the latter two being predominantly Islamic countries.

The claim on the land for Hinduism, however, is more subtle and different than that in the Middle East. Since Hinduism is itself a coalition of a number of religious perceptions, denominations and movements, the *hinduttva* movement, at least in theory, does not seek to suppress religious diversity itself but claims that all religious communities in India should see themselves culturally as part of the one Hinduness of India. Thus, the ideology accepts Sikhism and Jainism as part of the Hindu ethos. However, this means, in concrete terms, that Christians and Muslims should also become Hindu in their ethos, accept the validity and reality of Hinduism as the religion of India, and refrain from their own missionary activities to convert Hindus into their fold. Also resented by the nationalists are international linkages that Christians and Muslims use in their efforts to bring peoples into their brands of faith.

The issues are complex here. There is considerable sympathy among many for the reservations about the infusion of funds from outside the country for the Christian and Muslim missionary enterprises. There are indeed some unscrupulous mission agencies in the West and the Middle East that do fund missionary activities that use unethical methods of conversion. They also often misrepresent Hinduism and exploit the poverty of the masses.

However, there are Christians and churches in India that completely distance themselves from such activities but defend the rights of individuals to choose the religion to which they wish to belong. Christianity has been in India from at least about 250 CE and, despite all the ambiguities of its relationship with the colonizers who came later, has become one of the established religious paths of a significant number of Indians. In the same manner, Islam is a well-established religion of a significant percentage of the Indian population and there are Muslims and Muslim organizations that also unequivocally reject unethical and exploitative methods of conversion.

Buddhism, Sikhism and Jainism, which originated in India, while sharing much with Hinduism, arose as protest movements that distanced themselves from some of the basic foundations of Hindu social structure and wish to have the right to affirm a distinctive identity. Given the history and nature of all these many religious traditions, what implications are carried by the demand that all of them be part of the "Hinduness" of India?

Some see the emergence of this ideology as a necessary "wake-up call" to sections of Christians and Muslims to curtail their excessive missionary zeal and to respect the self-understanding of other religious traditions. Others accuse the ideology of being a pretext to prevent the Dalit, the oppressed outcastes, who are considered "untouchables" within the Hindu caste system, from escaping the oppressive clutches of the Hindu social hierarchy by embracing other religious paths. Many, also within the Hindu tradition, worry about the ideology's impact on questions of religious tolerance and freedom that are so much a part of the Indian ethos.

Periodic acts of violence on the part of Hindus and Muslims reached their peak when Hindu extremists pulled down the many centuries-old Babri Masjid in Ayodhya, an Islamic mosque, claiming that the mosque was standing on the location where there had been a Hindu temple. Ayodhya is a special place for the Hindus who claim it to be the birthplace of Ram, one of the main deities of Hinduism and believed by Hindus to be one of the many incarnations of God.

On another occasion, a local feud at a railway station turned into a major Hindu-Muslim confrontation when a Muslim gang set fire to a train bringing back pilgrims from Ayodhya. It resulted in the death of hundreds of Hindus; the counter-violence that ensued took the lives of over one thousand innocent Muslims. There have also been attacks on Christian churches and missionaries.

The issues here are complex because *hinduttva* is both a religious and a political ideology with all the ramifications that entails. All religious communities share some responsibility for the overall erosion of inter-religious relations in India. What is important to note is that here again a section of the Hindu community has begun to make an exclusive claim to the right to define the character of a landmass that is already occupied by peoples of different religious and cultural traditions. Religion thus has become inextricably bound up with social and political violence.

In neighbouring Sri Lanka, some sections of the Buddhist community lay claim to the land as the one that had been specially designated by the Lord Buddha as the *dammadeepa*, land specifically set aside for the preservation of the *Buddhadamma,* the Buddhist teachings. Once such claims are made, religious plurality becomes a problem and religions come to be embroiled in violence.

Religion, culture and identity

The illustrations above point to the close relationship between religion, culture and identity. Those tempted to see religion as some kind of spiritual compartment of life that can be isolated from the rest of what it means to be human miss the foundations on which most religious traditions are built. Such distinctions are sometimes used within Christianity in discussions on the indigenization the church and the inculturation of the gospel. But in reality when religious beliefs do play a significant role in a society, they inform the way the culture of the community expresses itself. In most situations culture is the manifestation of religious beliefs and religion is the nucleus of culture. In the Native American traditions, African religious traditions and religions of the tribal peoples, there is no such thing as a religion that is separate from culture or culture that can be separated from religion. Religion is the way of life.

Such close links may also be formalized in religious belief as in the case of Islam, which sees personal, family, social and political life as one reality that must be subjected to the revelation given to the Prophet. Therefore, the rulers are also the protectors and preservers of the religious tradition which forms the basis of all social relationships. In such an understanding, culture is the flowering of religious beliefs, and when that culture is under attack, the attack is experienced as one on religion itself. Different approaches to the relationship between religion and culture and the link between religion and political life are at the heart of misunderstandings between the "Christian" West and the Islamic world.

The "Western world" seeks to isolate religion and culture, and religion and state, often not quite recognizing that what is considered "neutral" culture and "secular" state are in fact founded on principles developed from the inspiration of the Jewish and Christian religious traditions. The torturous experience of the marriage between religion and state during the Middle Ages in Europe has driven Western determination to keep the two separate. It also finds that such separation, however tenuous, is an asset in religiously plural societies. The Muslim world, for its part, attempts to hold fast to the relationship between religion and state so that some of the high ideals and principles of religious faith will inform the political and cultural life of the nations concerned. Not all of them have been able to resolve the problems presented by the desire to organize national life on a single religious tradition when the nation itself has become religiously plural.

For our purposes what is important is to note the role that the close link between religion, culture and identity has in much of the violence we see today.

Identity and violence

The processes of globalization and population movements have begun to affect many dimensions of our identities. When I was invited in 1981 to work at the headquarters of the World Council of Churches in Geneva, my wife and I moved there with our three daughters, Dharshi, Niro and Anu, then aged 5, 3 and 1. When we left Sri Lanka we had some firm identity marks. We were Sri Lankans by nationality, Tamils by language and culture, Christians by faith. We stayed in Geneva for well over twenty years. The children went to the local school in the French section of Switzerland with German as the second language. Throughout this period we tried to maintain a Sri Lankan home in Geneva. We visited Sri Lanka and India as often as possible. As part of internalizing the Tamil culture the three girls learned the Indian classical dance, *bharathanatyam* and gave stage performances in a number of countries.

At school the children made friends with girls and boys from all parts of the world: Swiss, African, Asian, Middle Eastern, European, Latin American, North American and so on, because Geneva is home to some one hundred international organizations of different sizes. Nearly one third of the population of Geneva is made up to foreigners working in international organizations, multinational corporations, missions and embassies.

Little wonder that this has made an enormous dent on the identities with which our children found themselves. Today they are Swiss nationals; they speak French and English with greater fluency than their mother tongue; their outlook towards the world has radically changed in comparison with what it would have been had they remained in Sri Lanka. There are losses and gains. But what strikes me most is that while almost all other identities have come under much pressure, their religious identity is the one that has remained untouched. Their approach to religion has, of course, been tempered by the highly secularized Swiss society. But they are Christians, and they shall remain so unless for some reason they want to embrace another religious tradition. Even if some day they were to lose the connections with the church in which we worship, their religious identity will still be preserved intact.

I have given this illustration to show that in a complex and globalizing world today, where identities have begun to erode, it has become difficult to mobilize people on the basis of political ideologies, national identities and even ethnic/racial identities. No doubt, these identities do play a role in some conflicts. But religion has emerged in some parts of the world as the most effective tool for political and social mobilization and manipulation. Thus those who seek to mobilize people on the basis of Christian, Muslim, Hindu or Buddhist identities are not necessarily ardent followers of these religions and may not even be aware of their teachings. But they have understood the power of religious identity as a tool to fan the flames of violent confrontation.

Many conflicts that have little to do with actual confrontation between religions or religious communities are identified as religious conflicts. The conflict in Northern Ireland between "Protestants" and "Catholics" is an example of how religious identity functions as a mobilizing force. A conflict that is rooted in an intractable problem created by colonial history appears to be a purely religious conflict. The conflicts in former Yugoslavia, Sudan, Sri Lanka, Algeria, Fiji, the Philippines and Nigeria are also examples of religious identity playing a significant role in multi-faceted conflicts.

Therefore, it is important to look at the different roles that religions play in any specific conflict situation. Among others, five stand out:

- religion providing the group identity of communities that are in conflict over economic, social and political issues;
- religious sentiments being used as an instrument of mobilization in order to come to power or to expel a dictator or a government already in power;

- religious sentiment aggravating a conflict in which a specific minority group is marginalized or suppressed by a majority community;
- historical memory of religious persecution or suppression aggravating contemporary problems that have little to do with religious beliefs;
- a particular religion becoming part of a social, political or economic ideology and thus finding itself embroiled in ideological conflicts.

In fact a deeper analysis of each of these violent situations would show an array of ways in which religion comes to be associated with violence.

Can we say, then, that religions in themselves are free of violent tendencies? As has been said earlier, many have begun to ask whether there is something in the way religions are conceived and practised that carries a potential for violence and the inherent possibility of being manipulated for violent purposes.

Monotheism: a blessing or a threat?

In an inter-religious seminar I heard one of the Christian participants say that the greatest contribution that Judaism, Christianity and Islam have made to the world is monotheism. In fact from my young days I had been taught to believe that monotheism is a superior religious teaching. This teaching was accomplished with some emphasis in my own country of Sri Lanka to infuse us Christians with a sense of superiority over the Hindus, who were portrayed as polytheists, and the Buddhists who bypass the concept of God in their penetrating analysis of the human predicament.

There is also some interest in bringing the so-called Abrahamic faiths closer together, because they not only acknowledge the oneness of God but also claim relationship to a common ancestor. At first sight it would appear that to believe that the whole of humankind is under the loving care of one Reality would be a good starting point for building human relationships. But when we look back at history, these three religious traditions have had a very difficult time getting along with each other. Initial tensions that attended the separation of Christianity from Judaism, the European history of antisemitism, the holocaust, the conflict over the creation of the state of Israel, controversy over actions of the state of Israel, tensions over Jerusalem and so on plague this relationship. Recent Christian-Jewish dialogue has moved this relationship forward and helped to heal some of the wounds, but the relationship is still far from satisfactory.

Similarly, Christian-Muslim and Jewish-Muslim relationships have had a sorrowful history marked by armed conflicts, periods of suppression of one community by another, crusades and wars. In spite of the fact that in the Middle East peoples of these traditions have lived in harmony and in the dialogue of life for centuries, too much of the overall history of the monotheistic religions is written in blood.

The monotheism of each of these religious traditions appears to constitute the belief that there is only one God who revealed Godself to them in specific ways, and that "their" God is the creator and sustainer of the whole creation. In other words, much of the understanding of monotheism in these religions moved in the direction of making "their" God universal rather than in the direction of serving the one God whom all nations serve and worship – albeit under different names and with a variety of conceptions of who this God is.

No doubt, in deeper philosophical and theological reflections within these traditions the oneness of God has been spelt out to embrace the subtleties of the universality that such belief entails. But I always have believed that Christians paid only lip service to monotheism because they would have enormous difficulty in confessing that they as well as the Muslims, Hindus and Sikhs worship the one God. Thus, even though the oneness of God is confessed, in reality they are making allowances for the existence of Hindu, Muslim and Sikh gods.

There are, of course, a variety of conceptions of God in different religious traditions. They are indeed different from one another, and one does not have to agree or embrace any and all notions about God. However, the monotheistic religions have not drawn the radical consequences of their own belief in the oneness of God. If they truly believe God to be the creator and sustainer of all peoples, this must affect their relationship to each other and to others. Instead, monotheism has meant to each of these religious communities that God who is believed to have entered into a special relationship with their community or has given special revelation to them is the *only* God. In most schools of Christianity and Islam, all others are told to become part of their own fold in order to enter into a meaningful relationship with God. And in the eschatological visions of the Hebrew scriptures, all nations are expected finally to come to the Mountain of the Lord and acknowledge Yahweh as God.

Since these traditions see "their" God as the one God, there was no room for "other gods", or for anyone who believed that the Ultimate Reality could and indeed of necessity would be celebrated in a variety of names and forms. The overall result is that the so-called monotheistic religions have been, to varying degrees, the most exclusive and intolerant religions in religious history. And they have, far too often, taken the sword to defend their God, to execute God's promise or to promote their beliefs about God among the nations. They also have a long history of attributing violence to God and of seeing God to be on "their side" as they perpetrated violence on other peoples and nations.

In reality, the direct implication of strict monotheism should be that there is only one human family, and that all peoples have been seeking to relate to the one God in a variety of ways. A truly monotheistic faith would also affirm that God relates to, and loves, all peoples. Where one is not prepared to accept the consequences of that belief, monotheism can become a deadly asset.

Moreover, strong belief in monotheism has also led to the general ethos of believing that "one" is better than "many'. Here there is an interesting difference in the approach towards life and reality between the monotheistic traditions that originated in the Middle East region and other Asian religious traditions. In the monotheistic traditions the emphasis is on unity (oneness). Therefore, truth is one; there is only one way to salvation; there is only one true message. And those who differ (heretics) have to be eliminated or expelled. Truth is arrived at by exclusion of what does not belong. But most Asian religious traditions begin with the affirmation of the "manyness" of reality and seek to hold this diversity in harmony. The emphasis is not so much on removing what does not belong but on how all things can be helped to cohere.

The concept of harmony can also be abused. Some of the Asian religious traditions have produced unjust hierarchical structures that are defended on the pretext of maintaining social harmony. But the problem with emphasis on oneness is that it cannot handle plurality. And when one cannot handle plurality in a pluralistic situation, violence lurks nearby.

Relationships among the monotheistic religions and their relationship to other religions can never be put right unless the concept of monotheism is itself re-evaluated with searching questions as to its meaning, implications and application.

God is on our side

The belief that "God is on our side" is comforting, but it can also become a dangerous ideology. Dark night descends when a person or a nation confuses his, her or its thoughts and actions with those of God. The folk singer Bob Dylan's song from the late 1960s, "With God on Our Side", lifts up the dangers of co-opting God:

> Oh my name it is nothin'
> My age it means less,
> The country I come from
> Is called the Midwest;
> I's taught and brought up there
> The laws to abide,
> And that land that I live in
> Has God on its side...
>
> Oh the first world war, boys,
> It closed out its fate,
> The reason for fighting

I never got straight;
But I learned to accept it
Accept it with pride,
For you don't count the dead
When God's on your side...

But now we got weapons
Of the chemical dust;
If fire them we're forced to
Then fire them we must.
One push of the button
And a shot the world wide,
And you never ask questions
When God's on your side.

In a many dark hour
I've been thinkin' about this-
That Jesus Christ
Was betrayed by a kiss.
But I can't think for you
You'll have to decide
Whether Judas Iscariot
Had God on his side.

Four specific issues that contribute to the violent tendencies of monotheistic religious traditions call for closer attention.

Exclusive claims

Unlike traditional, tribal and ethnic religions, the three main monotheistic religions (Judaism, Christianity and Islam) are based on a belief in special revelations. The communities that receive revelations see themselves as in some sense "chosen', "special", "unique" or as having been entrusted with a message relevant to the whole world. In Judaism the revelation not only related to the Torah but also to a covenant relationship and a promise of a land in which that covenant relationship was to be worked out. In the case of Christianity, mainline theological tradition developed the idea that what was enacted in Christ was relevant to each and every person in the world. The Christ-event became the lens through which Christians perceived all of humanity. In the case of Islam, the revelation to the Prophet was the last and final revelation for the whole of humankind. Thus, all peoples of the world became the potential *umma* (Islamic faith community). The problems inherent in such beliefs need not be spelt out. Seeds of dissent, rivalry and violence are built into them.

The urge to engage in mission

With the exclusive claim comes, especially in the case of Christianity and Islam, the impetus for mission. Initially the momentum for mission comes from a genuine enthusiasm to share the richness and newness of the message that is experienced or regarded as relevant for all people. But soon missions become programmes of propagation of one's beliefs. A religion for the whole world needs to develop a strategy for world outreach. It needs mechanisms to deal with resistance. It needs to draw clear boundaries, well-defined doctrines and a powerful teaching authority to maintain the purity of the faith as the religious tradition is taken across new nations and cultures. And where necessary it should seek the help of ruling powers, and where possible collaborate with them, in order to get facilities necessary for the missionary effort.

Therefore it is no surprise that much of the spread of Christianity and Islam was accompanied by military conquests of kingdoms and empires. The unholy alliance between religious traditions and colonial powers, between the spread of religion and the expansion of the empires, dragged religious traditions deeply into war and violence. Some sections of the religious communities gave religious justification to such horrendous social evils as slavery, apartheid, untouchability and cultural and even literal genocides against indigenous peoples.

Violence and religious duty

Often violence is also built into theological thinking and religious duties laid out in religious traditions. Animal sacrifices and the spilling of the blood of an animal as atonement for one's sins are adopted by some of them. One of the theories of the significance of the death of Christ, atonement by the shedding of blood, is shown in a most abhorrent way in the much-discussed movie by director Mel Gibson, *The Passion of the Christ*. The film appears to suggest that Christ had to shed blood from every square inch of his body, undergo hideous torture and cruel death in order for God to extend God's forgiving love to people! It takes a stream of Christian piety and appears to present it as the Christian faith at the expense of the core Christian message of love and the challenge of discipleship. Christianity comes through as a bloody affair.

Laws within some of the religious traditions call for violence against offenders. Some encourage violence in order to defend the faith. During the Middle Ages, the church developed the concept of "holy war" to designate wars fought to redeem Christian holy sites in Jerusalem. The original meaning of the Islamic concept of jihad is "effort" or "struggle", the most important being the inner jihad for purity of the heart and the outer jihad of establishing justice. But historically the concepts of "holy war" in Christianity, "The Lord, strong and mighty" in the Hebrew scriptures and the "jihad" in Islam have found expression in all-out war and violence between religious communities. The association of religious beliefs, held by sections within larger religious communities, with suicide and terrorist attacks, state terrorism and warfare has brought even more ill repute to religious traditions. As a result, many see religions not as the solution but as the main part of the problem of violence.

From the above discussion we ought not to come to the conclusion that only those who follow monotheistic religions contribute to violence in the world. Far from it! Sri Lanka, Kampuchea, Vietnam, for instance, are "Buddhist" countries embroiled in intractable internal conflicts. Much of the violence in India today is associated with Hindu nationalism. The Hindu mythology, for instance, is full of war and violence, often committed by gods and goddesses themselves. Even though these myths are intended to depict the triumph of good over evil, extremists within Hinduism draw inspiration from them for the violence practised in our day.

Religion as a force for reconciliation and peace

If what we have discussed above were the only dimension of religions we would have an easy time. All that one would have to do is to ban them socially and legally, as one would ban organizations that promote hatred and violence. Happily religious history shows that religions have also played a significant role in creating a culture of peace and tranquillity. It has been said that humans are "religious animals". By this is meant that religions serve the role of controlling the violent instincts of human beings and channelling them into the service of justice, love, peace and reconciliation. Religious history abounds with saints and sages who became totally selfless and spent their whole lives in the service of others. Religions are replete with teachings that seek to direct the lives of individuals and communities in the ways of love and peace. They have built places of worship, rituals, teaching traditions and so on that seek to cultivate a spirit of harmony with all that is around them.

The question of religion and violence thus remains an enigma. Would a world without religious traditions, and the spiritual teachings they bring, be a less violent place? Are human beings without religious inspiration capable of developing values, principles and outlooks that would usher in a more peaceful world?

The ambiguities that surround the teachings and practice of religions are one of the biggest challenges we face today. Religions will either become spent spiritual forces that get manipulated by those in power to satisfy their base needs, or they may become spiritual forces that inform, correct, and lead societies in the ways of peace.

Will religions be able to meet the challenge of rampant violence that has engulfed our personal, social and political lives? The jury is still out on this issue.

Having looked at the question of religion and violence in general, it may be useful to turn our attention to the specific issue of war and violence in the Bible. Much of what has been said under religion and violence applies to the Bible as well. Therefore it would be more creative to look at the question of violence in the Bible with a view towards identifying different kinds of violence and relating them to contemporary situations. The word violence covers a wide variety of situations and responses. It would be useful to unpack all this so that we are better served when we come to the chapter that seeks to look for answers.

6. Violence and War in the Bible

When my daughters were of school age, they regularly attended Sunday school that would begin at the middle of the Sunday service and end about the same time the church service was brought to its close. On the way back home our children would tell us what they had been taught. It would give me a sense of the theology of the Sunday school teachers and the kind of religious sensitivities that were being inculcated in the class. From time to time I would gently add a few thoughts to help them not to "swallow" everything the Sunday school teacher said, but to develop a critical facility also in understanding and appropriating religious truths. It was a very delicate task. On the one hand, I did not want the children to internalize exclusive and self-righteous attitudes in the way they learned their religion; on the other, I did not want them to lose their confidence in the teachers.

I am aware that these days there are good Sunday school teaching materials and teachers who help the children to have an intelligent grasp of the biblical faith. It is not my intention here to create a caricature of a Sunday school teacher. But the "theology of the Sunday school" is a matter that continued to bother me because when I became an adult I myself had to unlearn quite a lot that I had learned at Sunday school.

The Bible became one of the issues. One of my daughters' Sunday school teachers had been insisting that the Bible is the inspired word of God and therefore everything that the Bible said was true. The teacher had also convinced the class that they must read the Bible every day.

One of my daughters had begun to read the Bible from the beginning.

One day she called out for me from her room. As I entered, I found her propped up against her pillow with the open Bible on her lap. I knew I was in for a theological conversation. She was reading the book of Joshua.

"It's terrible," she said, "It says that God was leading the people in war and destroying everyone in the land of Canaan."

It was no surprise, but I was pleased that at that moment she was objecting not so much to God, but to what the Bible had to say about God. I also heard the unsaid, "If this is what the Bible says about God, how can it be the inspired word of God?"

It took some time to tell her about the nature of the biblical material and who it was that was speaking about God in that passage, and why. She appeared to be satisfied once she knew the nature of the material she was reading.

Why would the Sunday school teacher insult the intelligence of his students by not explaining to them the nature of the material they were dealing with? I remembered how I had painfully to overcome the brainwashing I had about the Bible, before I rediscovered it as a book of life.

The truth of the matter is that the Bible is full of violence, and we Christians need help to read it intelligently.

Violence in the Bible

The Bible begins with the affirmation that God saw the universe that had been created "very good", but soon Genesis summarizes the human predicament in terms of alienation between God and human beings, and between human beings and nature (Gen. 3). This chapter is immediately followed by the story of the brutal murder of Abel by his brother Cain. The story is said to reflect the early struggle between the pastoral and agricultural ways of life. However, even though the story says that God held Cain accountable for his brother's murder, in fact it depicts Cain the murderer as the one who begins human civilization under the protection of God. In response to Cain's fear that he might himself be killed as a fugitive, God is presented as saying, "'Not so! Whoever kills Cain will suffer a seven-fold vengeance.' And the Lord put a mark on Cain, so that no one who came upon him will kill him" (Gen. 4:15).

Soon violence is also to be attributed to God:

Then the Lord saw that the wickedness of humankind was great in the earth, and that every inclination of the thoughts of their hearts was only evil continually. And the Lord was sorry that he had made the earth, and it grieved him to his heart. So the Lord said, "I will blot out from the earth the human beings I have created – people together with the animals and creeping things and the birds of the air, for I am sorry that I have made them. (Gen. 6:5-7)

This attribution of violence to God continues in much of the rest of the Bible. The devastation brought on Egypt, including the death of the first-born of Egypt, the destruction of the Egyptian army in the Red Sea, the conquest of Canaan, including the genocidal acts of wiping out whole tribes, are all depicted as acts done by, supported by or even required by God. The story of the conquest of Jericho, for instance, ends in this note:

> As soon as the people heard the trumpets, they raised a great shout, and the wall fell down flat; so the people charged straight ahead into the city and captured it. Then they devoted to destruction by the edge of the sword all in the city, both men and women, young and old, oxen, sheep and donkeys (Josh. 6:20-21).

All the wars that are won are presented as acts of the Lord himself leading the people into battle, and all wars lost are God's punishment for the sins of the people.

Contemporary scholars question the historicity of most of the stories and draw our attention to what the writers are trying to convey to us through these accounts. What bothered me about the theology of that particular Sunday school teacher was that he had not helped my daughter to deal with this horrendous picture of God that so much of the Bible presents. The stories of violent warfare in the Bible should be read in their historical context. They are part of the prevalent practice of tribes in the deserts of the Middle East constantly waging war against each other to control the few, scattered fertile portions of the land on which the survival of the tribes depended. It should come as no surprise that the gods of such tribes are represented as deities who give them victory in conquests of the fertile lands. It is also to be understood that the biblical stories and historiography are theological readings and interpretations of events by a particular people, with all the promises and problems such readings entail. If we do not understand these events as people's interpretation of their history, we will end up with an image of a bloodthirsty God.

But what is important for our present topic is that one of the prominent dimensions of the biblical image of God becomes closely associated with domination, conquest and relentless violence.

As was said earlier, contemporary Christian thinking is also delving deeply into the impact of the concept of blood sacrifice, which is at the heart of both testaments. What relation does it have to the psychology of violence? The requirement to shed animal blood as the symbol of reconciliation between God and a person who had sinned, it is claimed, justifies the shedding of blood as a religious duty. This basic principle is worked out in Christian theology in at least one major theory of atonement which claims that Jesus had to die a violent death in order to placate God's anger over the sins of humankind. Jesus' "sacrificial death", "shedding of blood for our sins" and "paying the price of sin" are common themes in Christian hymnody, piety and theology. In the controversy conducted on television networks in the US over the level of violence in Mel Gibson's *The Passion of the Christ*, mentioned earlier, a number of preachers from one stream of the Christian tradition defend the film by insisting that God could never have forgiven their sins but for the blood that was shed in that way, and in that quantity.

The second area where such violence plays a major role lies in the way some biblical imagery and theology depict the problem of evil in terms of violent and ongoing "battles" between good and evil, light and darkness, God and Satan. Hence, the eschatological vision in Revelation presents a cosmic battle between the powers of evil and good, in which the powers of evil, after a violent struggle, are conquered, overcome, subdued and eventually abolished by God and God's angels. Power, conquest and domination take centre stage in these images.

Violence is also clearly present in Christian images of mission and evangelization of the world. Military language like "conquering the world for Christ", "deployment of missionaries", "mission strategy", "soldiers of Christ", and "evangelistic crusades" are still very much in use in some sections of the church.

Several years ago, the then-general secretary of the WCC, Emilio Castro, made a pastoral visit to Nigeria. One of the matters that precipitated the need for this visit was the violence that had broken out in northern Nigeria between Christians and Muslims. Christians had been killed in inter-religious, inter-tribal violence and many churches had been set on fire. Many Muslims had also been killed in Christian reprisals. Castro's mission was to show solidarity with those affected and to appeal for peaceful ways of resolving the conflict. The churches received him with much fanfare. The largest church gathering organized to receive him, to Castro's embarrassment, opened with the hymn,

> Onward Christian soldiers, marching as to war,
> With the cross of Jesus going on before!

Clearly, those who organized the liturgy had not put this hymn in on purpose. Perhaps they wanted to begin the service with a robust hymn. They had perhaps failed to recognize the militarism that had infested our faith and piety.

It is little wonder, then, that parts of the history of the church are written in blood. The burning of heretics, inquisitions, crusades, holocaust, slavery and the ruthless violence that accompanied the establishment of Christianity in Latin America, Africa and Australia are all part of the history of Christianity.

Religious language and imagery used by some of the leadership in the US administration during the Iraqi war draws its inspiration from this strand of the Bible. They confirm the image many people of other religious traditions have of Christianity as a religion that promotes domination, war and violence.

Christians, therefore, have much homework to do. Is Christianity really a religion based on violence and bloodshed?

The other side of the Bible

While the Bible is full of violent episodes, there is also another stream within the Bible that resists war and violence as against God's will and purpose. God is also presented as loving, forgiving and compassionate (Ps. 103), demanding righteousness and justice in human affairs. It is in the Bible that we encounter the revolutionary concept of the Jubilee year in which slaves are set free, debts are forgiven and lands taken in pledge are returned to the original owners. Whether it was actually practised in history is questionable, but the concept is very much in keeping with the biblical vision of God's solidarity with the poor and the oppressed.

Clear and unambiguous prohibition of killing is part of the ten commandments, and there are detailed provisions against social and economic violence in the form of relentless advocacy for justice, especially in favour of the peoples at the margins of the society. The prophet Amos recalls God's displeasure with the violence perpetrated not only by Israel and Judah but also its neighbouring nations (Amos 1-2).

Significantly, all the eschatological visions in the Old Testament deal with cessation of violence and a state of reconciliation between nations, between God and human beings, as well as in and with the natural world. In Isaiah's vision,

> The wolf shall live with the lamb, the leopard shall lie down with the kid... The cow and the bear shall graze, and their young shall lie down together; and the lion shall eat straw like an ox... They will not hurt or destroy on all my holy mountain; for the earth will be full of the knowledge of the Lord as the waters cover the sea. (Isa. 11:6-9)

Micah sees a vision of an absolute reversal of the way nations relate to one another:

> He shall judge between many peoples, and arbitrate between strong nations far away; they shall beat their swords into ploughshares, and their spears into pruning hooks; nation shall not lift up sword against nation, and neither shall they learn war any more. (Micah 4:3)

What more can we ask for?

Jesus, the teacher

Christians are, of course, specifically interested in the teachings of Jesus on violence and nonviolence. There is considerable discussion among New Testament scholars on how much we do in fact know about the teachings of Jesus, because the gospels were written decades after his death and it is commonly agreed that each one of the gospel writers seeks to provide his own interpretation of the life and significance of Christ. We need, therefore, to deal with Jesus as he comes to us in the presentations of the gospel writers. There is, however, no reason to doubt the overall picture that the gospel narratives present concerning Jesus' attitude to violence.

There are also considerable differences in the scholarly assessment of Jesus' attitude to the Roman empire and his relationship to the Zealots who advocated a violent overthrow of Roman power. It is clear that some Zealots were members of the band of disciples that followed Jesus in his ministry. At one point Jesus is presented as saying that he has come "not to bring peace but a sword" (Matt. 10:34), and in chapter 11, Matthew again presents Jesus as reproaching unrepentant cities in harsh language (Matt. 11:20-24).

The bulk of the New Testament witness, however, presents Jesus as one who advocated radical nonviolence.

> You have heard that it was said, "An eye for an eye and a tooth for a tooth." But I say to you, do not resist an evildoer. But if anyone strikes you on the right cheek, turn the other also... You have heard that it was said, "You shall love your neighbour and hate your enemy." But I say to you, love your enemies and pray for those who persecute you, so that you may be children of your Father in Heaven; for he makes his sun to rise on the evil and on the good, and sends rain on the righteous and the unrighteous... Be perfect, therefore, as your heavenly Father is perfect. (Matt. 5:38-45,48)

Matthew also presents Jesus as espousing total nonviolence in his account of Jesus' arrest and trial. When one of the persons who was with Jesus drew a sword to defend him, Jesus is reported to have said, "Put your sword back into its place; for all who take the sword will perish by the sword" (Matt. 26:52).

Study of the life of the early church shows that the church, as it emerged into a new religious tradition separated from its Jewish moorings, basically espoused a nonviolent stance in its relationship to the Roman empire. Even though that empire had begun an active persecution of the church for fear that those who followed "the Way" were disloyal to Rome, the church's nonviolent stance appears to have held until its whole ethos changed with the conversion of the Emperor Constantine. The political power and material wealth that came with the status of Christianity as the official religion of the Roman empire was to change its attitude to violence and nonviolence.

The discussion above shows that the Bible is a double-edged sword. It could be used to justify war and violence or to argue for total nonviolence; to present a God who is on the side of the conquerors leading them into battle or a God whose compassion never ends and who challenges us to be on the side of justice and righteousness.

But what impresses me in reading the Bible is that it is also a useful source to isolate the different kinds and levels of violence. Among others, seven particular kinds of violence stand out in the biblical narratives.

Violence as part of human nature arising out of jealousy, fear or hatred

It is quite fascinating to try to reflect on what the writers of the book of Genesis were trying to convey to us in the way they have conceived and ordered the first few narratives in their opening chapters.

First there was creation, which God found to be very good (Gen. 1-2). Then comes the story of human self-assertion, often described as the "fall" which, at least in traditional Christian theology, is presented as the story of the state of human alienation with God and the rest of nature. The third story, which is intended as the story of the beginning of human civilization, is set in the context of a murder scene, of

Cain killing his own brother, with all the intrigues and wickedness of such a brutal murder.

This story inspires us to raise a basic question, namely, whether human beings are naturally and inherently violent. The study booklet prepared in relation to the WCC's Decade to Overcome Violence *(Why Violence? Why Not Peace?)*, lifts up the ambiguous relations we humans have with violence (p.6):

– Violence repels us, but violence also attracts us.
– Violence alarms us, but violence also entertains us.
– Violence destroys us, but violence also protects us.

Today, the level of violence tolerated as "entertainment" is simply mind-boggling. The movies *Terminator*, *Star Wars*, *Matrix* (to name just a few) are box office hits. They were so much in demand, and made such big money, that the producers had to come up with sequels containing even more violence. When we cannot any longer make even super-human beings do sufficient violence to entertain us, the producers come up with all kinds of aliens and non-human creatures that would enact devastation on a much larger scale.

What is even more troubling is the violence that has been introduced into children's television programmes. In my younger days I was a fan of cartoon films, Pluto and Goofy being my favourite characters. They had a way of helping us laugh at ourselves. Goofy exposed human vanity in such a good-natured way! Tom and Jerry were quite fascinating because they depicted how the weak (Jerry, the mouse) could outsmart the powerful (Tom, the cat) with wit and wisdom. But gradually more and more violence has been introduced into Tom and Jerry so that Jerry's antics today have reached levels of violence that is almost repulsive. What is more, our sympathies have now moved from Jerry to Tom who was originally meant to be on the wrong side of the fence!

When it comes to the use of violence as entertainment for children, nothing is more glaring than computer games. Many parents who avoid buying toys that promote violence for their children get defeated when it comes to computer games, because what goes on the palm-held screen is not so obvious and visible. Most of the games are nothing more than training to kill. Many contemporary events like the Gulf war and sniper shootings are reproduced as computer games so that children "enjoy" themselves shooting down Iraqi soldiers or innocent bystanders.

Much more could be said here, but the basic question is whether the story of Cain and Abel tells us something profound about the nature of human beings: that we are naturally violent and are inclined to use and even relish violence as a way of life as long as it does not threaten our own lives.

There have been considerable studies on the psychology of violence because aggression, anger, hatred and their external expression in different forms of violence are no doubt part of human behaviour. Thus in a court of law those who commit violence that defies reason, such as killing one's own children, are subjected to psychiatric examination to determine whether they were in full control of themselves when the act of violence was committed. The emotional state of anger can be provoked by actions of others and by the evocation of memories that makes one lose control of oneself. Some scholars maintain that a percentage of the human population is biologically and bio-chemically prone towards violence. Neurologists have studied the role of brain functions in aggression and anger leading to violent episodes. Still others have searched for the relationship between violence and instinctive behaviour.

Another line of enquiry has been whether violence is learned socially. It is believed that those who are exposed to violence internalize it and reproduce it when triggered to do so. The socialization of violence through toys, television programmes, movies and computer games and so on has grown so much that the children of our day are brought up largely in a culture of violence.

As in many other fields, there is no agreement among scholars on whether the source of violence is natural, instinctive, biochemical or a socially learned behaviour. More than one factor may be at play and in any case human beings are so complex that they do not respond in the same way to given situations. Even the same person may not have the same response to similar stimulations on two different occasions.

What is interesting about the Bible is that it is very open about this kind of violence. In the Psalms, for instance, psalmists give full vent to their aggressive feelings, anger, hatred, and they call upon God to deal out avenging violence on behalf of the offended ones:

> Pour out your indignation upon them,
> and let your burning anger overtake them.
> May their camp be a desolation;
> let no one live in their tents...
> Add guilt to their guilt;
> may they have no acquittal from you.
> Let them be blotted out of the book of the living
> let them not be enrolled among the righteous. (Ps. 69:24-28)

Another dimension of violence in the Bible has to do with vengeance. Psalm 137 has a moving scene. Jerusalem had been captured and partly destroyed and a section of the people had been taken in captivity to Babylon (present-day Iraq). Some of the good-natured persons among their captors asked of some of the captives, "Sing us one of the songs of Zion!"

This brings back painful memories: "By the rivers of Babylon- there we sat down and wept when we remembered Zion... How could we sing the Lord's song in a foreign land?" Soon this anguish turns into a cry for vengeance:

> O daughter Babylon, you devastator!
> Happy shall they be who pay you back
> what you have done to us!
> Happy shall they be who take your little ones
> and dash them against the rock!

Troubling and all too human as it is, the cry for vengeance plays a significant role in present-day conflicts. The Middle East is perhaps the most obvious example. Every suicide bomb is responded to in a spirit of vengeance with retaliatory killings. And every retaliatory killing is answered with further suicide bombings. When vengeance is the motivation, violence runs in a cycle.

In the United States the attack on the Twin Towers and the Pentagon led, according to the polls, to a near national call for vengeance. Somebody had to be bombed, and soon, in order to placate the outrage and anger of the majority of the population. Leadership that did not retaliate with much greater force would be considered weak and ineffective. As a result, more innocent people were killed in Afghanistan than were killed in the Twin Towers. The sense of outrage was so great that people supported the invasion of Iraq when there seemed to be no credible reason to do so.

There were of course many in the United States, Israel and several other warring countries in Asia and Africa, who saw vengeance as self-defeating and who opposed generalized retribution in response to criminal acts. But they always remain a minority, and the major news channels would seldom call them to discuss the issue.

Violence as judgment and punishment

The second type of violence we encounter has to do with judgment and punishment. Already in the Garden of Eden, God is presented as handing out punishments to Adam, Eve and the serpent. More serious punishment follows in the story of the flood, when God decides to destroy everything that was created except a nucleus of people and animals to repopulate the earth.

Next, calamity falls on Sodom and Gomorrah. The presentation of the story of the destruction of Sodom and Gomorrah is quite interesting. Abraham protested to God on God's decision to destroy the twin cities: "Will you indeed sweep away the righteous with the wicked?" asked Abraham. "Suppose there are fifty righteous within the city; will you then sweep away the place and not forgive it for the fifty righteous who are in it?" Abraham told God that a general destruction of the good and the wicked alike would bring ill repute to God: "Shall not the judge of all the earth do what is just?" God promised to forgive the city if fifty righteous persons were found. Frustrated with his inability to come up with that number of righteous, Abraham bargains with God for forty-five, and then for thirty. Eventually Abraham beats God down to a mere ten righteous, but to no avail.

The story is instructive because it attempts to show that there is some kind of justice in God's violent acts of judgment. The writer wants to convince us that there were none who were righteous in those cities (!), and since they would not listen to good advice God was left with little choice but to rain down fire on them.

Much of the Bible is based on the assumption that evil has to be destroyed and those who do wrong individually and collectively have to be punished. So much so that whenever Israel appeared to go astray from God or from the observance of the Torah, prophets gave strong warnings of impending punishment. And whenever Israel suffered a great calamity like a defeat in battle, or being over-run by other nations and taken captive, they saw these as punishments they had brought on themselves for their sins. In this view, evil always needs to be punished.

As we have seen earlier, this theme is developed in great detail in the New Testament in Revelation. The struggle here between good and evil is of cosmic proportions. Evil had to be put down with whatever violence it took.

One of the major theories of the work of Christ developed by the apostle Paul is that through his death and resurrection Christ overcame and banished the principalities and powers (1 Cor. 15).

I was quite fascinated with the US administration's unrelenting use of the word "evil" in the period immediately following Nine-Eleven and in the task of convincing the nation of the need to invade Iraq. The primary description of bin Laden and Sadam Hussein was that they were evil. Al-Qaeda was evil; Sadam's rule was evil; we are in a struggle to overcome and destroy evil. Given the religious formation of much of the population of the United States, nothing could have made more sense. Evil must be dealt with and destroyed. That's what God does in the Bible!

The way God is said to govern the universe also becomes the pattern for human governance. Detailed laws were developed to deter and where necessary punish those who broke the laws of society; these measures included capital punishment. Today there is considerable discussion on the place and role of punishment in social governance. At one time severe corporal punishment of children to keep them in line was universally accepted; today it is frowned upon. The complex of circumstances that drive a person to become anti-social or a law-breaker are being recognized; nations and peoples are deeply divided over the nature, role and kinds of punishments as well as the administration of capital punishment.

We must recognize, however, that the direct correlation between offence and punishment is a matter on which there are also second thoughts in the Bible. There are passages and sentiments that run counter to the predominant idea of violence as the only possibility in countering and deterring violence. In Psalm 103 we find a moving vision of God as one whose compassion over-rides the demands of justice:

> He does not deal with us according to our sins,
> nor repay us according to our iniquities.
> For as the heavens are high above the earth,
> so great is his steadfast love toward those who fear him;
> as far as the east is from the west,
> so far he removes our transgressions from us...
> For he knows how we are made;
> he remembers that we are dust. (vv.10-12,14)

Similar sentiments in relation to the whole nation are found in Hosea. The nation had moved away from God, and their unfaithfulness to the covenant had become unbearable to God. Yet God's compassion and loving kindness surpassed the inclination to punish:

> How can I give you up, Ephraim?
> How can I hand you over, O Israel?...
> My heart recoils within me;
> my compassion grows warm and tender.
> I will not execute my fierce anger;

> I will not destroy Ephraim;
> for I am God and no mortal,
> the holy one in your midst,
> and I will not come in wrath. (11:8-9)

The book of Job was quite revolutionary for its time, for it advances the discussion even further to discuss the possibility of great calamity falling on persons who did not deserve it. Even though it does not give definitive answers, it succeeds in making a dent on the prevalent belief, supported by Job's friends, that there is a direct correlation between suffering and God's judgment.

In the presentations of Jesus in the synoptic gospels, Jesus appears to be among the rabbis of his time who sought to begin an internal debate within their own religious tradition on the role of law in society and the place of understanding, forgiveness and healing in dealing with offenders. But his ministry of announcing God's forgiveness to the undeserving became deeply controversial. The gospels present him as arguing for the practicality of overcoming evil with good by refusing to pay back evil for evil. Jesus appears to hold that one who truly loves God and one's neighbour would be willing to break the cycle of violence by "absorbing" the hurt or the wrong done – which he describes as forgiveness. Forgiveness in Jesus' teaching brings healing on all sides and makes it possible to begin anew (Matt. 6:14-15).

Popular sentiment, however, runs against even trying this possibility. I am always fascinated by television interviews with the relatives of those who have been murdered under one circumstance or another. With very rare exceptions, almost all the relatives of the victims argue that the perpetrator of the crime must be given not life imprisonment but a death sentence so that they would have "closure", and "justice" would be done. The television interviewers, for some reason, always track down the relevant relative to ask this same question, "life" or "death", and receive the same answer, "death", because it seems to confirm their own views on the matter. On a rare occasion, when someone says that they are not looking for the death penalty because the situation will not be remedied by the state engaging in another killing, the interviewer looks at that person as if he or she had just arrived from Mars! We earthlings are supposed to call for revenge!

Following 11 September, there was a near nationwide cry in the USA for revenge, and a vast majority supported the heavy bombing of Afghanistan, despite the large number of innocent people being killed as "collateral damage". One of the most moving things that happened at that time was the formation of a coalition of relatives of Nine-Eleven victims who were against revenge and indiscriminate bombing of a country that was already in ruins and submerged in poverty through decades of conflict. Some of them even visited Afghanistan to express their solidarity with the innocent victims. They had only a passing mention in the mainstream media. Media prefer fireworks!

The appropriate use and role of violence in the course of social governance and in the administration of justice remains caught up in a divisive and inconclusive debate.

Violence as structured oppression

When the Hebrew historians sat down to write their "history" they made the liberation of the Hebrew slaves from Egypt and especially the giving of the Torah on Mount Sinai the focal points of their story. There is considerable debate on the historicity of several episodes in the Hebrew and Christian scriptures because much of the Bible was written long after the events, and the writers of the books of the Bible are more interested in interpretation of the faith that sustained the community rather than literal history. In any case all events come to us as reported from the perspective of the "historian".

However, our own interest here is that in the story of the Hebrew slaves in Egypt we are introduced to yet another dimension of violence, namely, violence as the structured oppression of people.

According to the biblical narratives, when Joseph the Israelite, sold by his brothers as a slave to Egyptian traders, found favour with the king and rose to a powerful position in Egypt, many of the families of his brothers eventually came to settle down in the land. Eventually Joseph and his brothers died, "But the Israelites were fruitful and prolific; they multiplied and grew exceedingly strong, so that the land was filled with them" (Ex. 1:1-7).

Structured violence against them began "when a new king arose in Egypt who did not know Joseph". The prosperous minority in the land was seen as an eventual threat: "Look, the Israelite people are more numerous and more powerful than we," said the king. "Come, let us deal shrewdly with them, or they will increase, and in the event of a war, join our enemies and fight against us and escape from the land" (Ex. 1:8-14.) This fear of the power of the minority led the Egyptians to develop structural procedures that began to oppress the Hebrews as a group.

They became slave labourers under hard task-masters, but this did not contain the population growth. Eventually, to check the growth of their numbers, the king ordered the midwives to kill all Hebrew male children at birth.

Unfortunately, such a story is not unfamiliar in our day. Structured oppression of minority groups and even attempts to eliminate them is part of our contemporary history. Many of the internal conflicts and wars in our day have to do with one ethnic, tribal, religious or national group oppressing another, or a group that is so oppressed taking up arms to assert its rights. Minority-majority conflicts rage in several countries such as for example Sri Lanka, Myanmar (Burma), India, Tibet, Sudan, Algeria, Iran, Iraq, Turkey, Nigeria, Spain, Ethiopia, Northern Ireland, Congo, Ivory Coast. Actual "ethnic cleansing" reaching genocidal proportions also has been attempted in our day in Germany (against the Jewish people), in Turkey (against the Armenians), in the former Yugoslavia (against the Muslims), in Rwanda (against the Tutsi), in Kampuchea (Cambodia) and other places. The fear of changing the demographic balance prevents Israel from granting Palestinians the right of return to homes and villages they fled during the wars. In some Islamic countries severe restrictions are in place regarding the rights of religious minorities.

Another form of structured oppression is dictatorship by a political party (as was the case, for instance, in the former Soviet Union) or a military dictator as in Argentina, Chile and several other countries in Latin America, Asia and Africa.

Structured social violence can also take place on other grounds. Some of the most glaring examples have been apartheid in South Africa, slavery in the United States, caste discrimination in India, where structured social violence was given religious and legal legitimacy. Even after legal sanctions are removed the violence in many places continues in the form of racism, casteism and so on.

Today we have been made aware of the way in which almost all societies have built structures that oppress women. Sexism in general is an abiding problem. More glaring is specific violence against women in wife-beating, killing of female infants, rape, dowry deaths, selling into prostitution and similar practices. Other forms of violence that are much in the news are homophobia and violence against children. Child slavery, child labour, child soldiers and child prostitution are phrases that denote the predicament of many millions in our day.

The problem with this discussion is that it can be an endless litany of woes. And I am sure that in my descriptions of the nations in relation to oppression of minorities many are missing, and some would be offended that they were mentioned while other glaring cases of human-rights violations are ignored. What we find here in each category are meant to be examples. You, the reader, will need to add or subtract countries and situations under each category. The main point being argued here is that violence is not only about guns and bombs, and it does not happen only when there is bloodletting. Violence is insidious and may become systemic; the less obvious it is, the more menacing it is.

Today there is also increased awareness and interest in economic violence, where the basic right to life is denied to millions of people in the way economic life is organized between and within nations. Peoples, and even nations, are excluded, marginalized and even considered disposable. Here again, violence and unjust economic structures are often given legitimacy by laws and agreements. Most people do not even see the culture of violence that is so pervasive in the economic field.

One of the strengths of the Bible is that it recognizes political, economic and social violence for what it is. In the writings of the Bible, especially in the prophets, we find unrelenting determination to expose it and to challenge those in power to deal with it. In relation to the Hebrew slaves in Egypt, God is presented as addressing Moses with these words: "I have observed the misery of my people who are in Egypt; I have heard their cry on account of their task masters. Indeed I know their suffering, and I have come down to deliver them..." (Ex. 3:7-8a). By using the four verbs, "observed", "heard", "know" and "come down", the writer seeks to create an atmosphere of impatience and a sense of urgency on the part of God. Much against his own will, Moses was pressed into service to liberate the Hebrew slaves from their task-masters.

There is no need to recount here the constant call for social and economic justice in the prophetic tradition. Amos's scathing criticism of the rich and powerful oppressors, Isaiah's call to care for the widows, the fatherless, the poor and the marginalized, Jeremiah's condemnation of political and religious leaders who say "peace, peace" when there was no political, religious or social harmony, and Jesus' announcement that he had come "to bring good news to the poor... and to let the oppressed go free..." – these are but a few isolated examples of the constant and tireless call in the Bible to reject violence and embrace justice in its place.

The prophet Micah sums up all of this in the much-quoted passage where he contrasts formal religion with what God actually requires of us: "He has told you, O mortal, what is

good; and what does the Lord require of you but to do justice, and to love kindness, and to walk humbly with your
God?" (6:8).

Violence as warfare

The Bible, as mentioned earlier, is full of narratives concerning warfare. We have already discussed the issue to some
extent, and therefore all that we need do here is to recognize
that there are a considerable number of groups, within both
Judaism and Christianity, which see in this an implied legitimacy to resorting to war as a means of resolving problems.
Or one might say that the presence of so much warfare in
what is considered by some to be the revealed or inspired
scriptures blinds them to the reality of the horrible violence
that wars entail. Their moral consciousness and their spiritual
sensitivities are blunted by the images of God leading the
people into battle. The image of the almighty and all-power-
ful God has also had the effect that many Christians and even
churches are willing to take sides with, condone, justify or in
other ways tolerate dictatorial rulers and governments.

Violence in resistance and liberation

The discussions above bring us immediately into another
difficult area in our consideration of the Bible and violence,
namely, the use of violence to resist injustice, oppression and
dictatorships. One of the troubling dimensions of the presentation of God in the Bible, as said earlier, is the attribution of
violent actions to God in the course of freeing the people of
Israel. The many plagues God is said to have sent on the
Egyptians culminate in the death of the first-born sons of
Egypt and the destruction of the Egyptian army in the sea.
Much more violence is attributed to God in the battles that
the Hebrews had to wage as they worked their way towards
the "land flowing with milk and honey". According to the
biblical narratives, the conquest of the land itself was
attended by violence of genocidal proportions. Seen from the
Canaanite standpoint, it would have been a brutal invasion of
their land.

Scholars of the Hebrew scriptures point out that the biblical picture of the occupation of the land is overly stylized. In reality, it is claimed by archaeologists and other scholars that the Hebrew settlement in the Canaanite land was gradual, long-term and that there were many alliances and much more assimilation than the biblical narrators would have us believe. But here again our primary interest is with the issue of violence, and specifically with the place of violence in the struggle for liberation and justice.

It appears that the biblical stories, with the exception of a strand in Jesus' own teaching, appear to see violence in the course of liberation as justified. In the book of Revelation, as seen earlier, the struggle between good and evil, between the temporal and spiritual powers, between God and Satan, is presented as a necessary climax for the ushering in of the reign of God over all of life.

In view of the advocacy in the Bible of "just violence" on the one hand and "nonviolence" on the other, the use of violence in resistance movements remains a much-debated issue. The Nazi regime in Germany produced the classical case in which Christians had to take sides either to support the regime (including by remaining silent) or to resist it actively.

For Dietrich Bonhoeffer, resisting the Nazi regime became a matter of Christian faith and discipleship. Therefore, he terminated his privileged research position at the Union Theological Seminary in New York and returned to his native Germany, to join in resistance and eventually to participate in a clandestine plot to assassinate Hitler. The plot was discovered, and the Nazis hanged Bonhoeffer. Today Bonhoeffer is considered a modern martyr, and his actions are cited by moral theorists as an example of "how Christians could undertake violent actions for just cause and how occasionally they are constrained to break the law for a higher purpose".[1] Reinhold Niebuhr, who was a colleague of Bonhoeffer at Union Seminary, and who began his carrier as a

---

[1] Jürgensmeyer, *Terror in the Mind of God*, p. 24.

pacifist, also came to the view that there may be situations in which violence may be necessary for a just cause.

The issue has resurfaced in our day with regard to the "positive" use of violence, for example, by an armed contingent of the United Nations, to prevent massacre of innocent peoples. The tragedies in Rwanda and Bosnia, for example, are cited as instances where limited and well-directed violence or armed intervention could have saved the lives of thousands of innocent victims.

There are, however, many Christians who believe that any use of violence would breed only more violence, and who maintain that we should work harder on developing measures to predict, prevent and manage disputes and on finding peaceful ways of resolving conflicts.

Christians also disagree on the legitimate use of violence in the course of liberation struggles. The struggle against the apartheid regime in South Africa and against the brutal dictatorships in Latin America (where thousands of dissidents simply "disappeared") provided the stage for much discussion within the ecumenical movement on the right of peoples to take up arms to liberate themselves from oppressive regimes. While some still opt for nonviolent resistance, others insist on allowing the oppressed to decide on the means of the struggle that is appropriate in a given situation.

Yes and no

The World Council of Churches has struggled with this question from its inception in 1948. Following several stages of debate within its programme on Church and Society, an important statement was made in 1973 under the title, "Violence, Nonviolence and the Struggle for Social Justice". Without itself taking a stance on the issue, it summarized the state of the debate for study by the churches in the following affirmations:

- Nonviolent action is the only way that is consistent with our obedience to Jesus Christ.
- However, there may be extreme situations where violent resistance may become a Christian duty, and in such cir-

cumstances Christians must follow principles like those enunciated for "just wars".

- This is being discussed because violence seems to be unavoidable in some situations where non-violence does not appear to be a viable option.

The report also identified kinds of violence that Christians must vehemently resist:

- violent causes like conquest of a people, race or class by another;
- unjustified violence such as holding hostages, torture, deliberate and indiscriminate killing of non-combatants.

Again, much of the emphasis was on ways of avoiding conflicts by building a culture of peace and dialogue.

While this has been the generally held position within the ecumenical movement, we must ask whether we need to go further in the light of contemporary developments. We shall return to this discussion in the final chapter.

Forms of violence

What is remarkable about the Bible is its remarkable honesty about the nature of human life. It does not attempt to sweep human weakness under the carpet. It is full of violence and of the search for justice and peace, because they are part of being human and much of what our lives are all about. One of the results of looking at the Bible and violence has been a heightening of our awareness of the range of violence that exists and the complexity of addressing its many manifestations. In addition to overt acts of violence, like killing a person or engaging in warfare, there are other forms of violence that need to be addressed.

- structural violence, where social, political, cultural structures oppress, segregate, exclude or marginalize groups of people;
- economic violence, where economic life is organized in a way that denies even the basic needs of people;
- social violence, where forces like racism and sexism exclude peoples on the basis of colour, gender, caste, ethnicity and so on;

- domestic violence, where women and children are abused or treated brutally within established relationships;
- psychological violence, where persons or groups of persons in an institution, or in a society in general, are kept intimidated, deprived of dignity and live in fear;
- moral violence, where the brutal force of the state or a dominant group denies peoples' human rights or the right to peoplehood;
- violence of warfare, undertaken for any number of reasons.

Within the ecumenical movement, therefore, there is a general concern about a "culture of violence" that is expressed in a variety of forms and places.

Before we leave this section we turn to deal with one other form of violence that occupies much of our thinking these days: terrorism.

Terrorism

The incidents of 11 September have brought into greater focus the question of terrorism as a form of violence, and of the religious and moral issues involved in suicide attacks, in which one takes one's own life and those of others in order to make a statement. The perpetrators of these acts consider themselves as martyrs, laying down their lives for a just cause. It is difficult to arrive at a definition of terrorism that would be acceptable to all, because what one group considers a "terrorist act" is seen by another as "liberation struggle" or even as "martyrdom".

The Oxford English Reference Dictionary defines terrorism as "the systematic use of violence and intimidation to coerce government or community, especially into acceding to specific political demands". One of the troubling features of contemporary terrorist acts is that they appear to seek to achieve maximum casualties among unarmed, innocent civilians. Clearly such terrorist and suicide attacks on innocent people are condemned by all religious traditions. There is no warrant for these actions in any body of religious scripture.

"Terrorism", however, is not a new phenomenon. Destruction of government property, derailing of trains, ambushing representatives of the government have been part of the national independence struggle in many colonized countries. Over the past several decades there have been numerous terrorist incidents perpetrated by people who demand attention to specific issues and grievances. On the whole, they have been confined within national borders.

Three developments have made peoples and governments sit up and take greater notice of this issue. First, today terrorism is no longer confined to national boundaries. There appear to be international networks at work that coordinate their activities across borders. In relation to the attacks on the Twin Towers, for instance, it would appear from media reports that the decision was made in Afghanistan, funds were channelled through the nations in the Gulf, cells were formed in Europe and pilot training was completed in the United States. Second, modern technologies and communication systems normally used by governments are now also readily available to these groups. And third, they appear to have access to considerable funding.

September 11th and the conflict in the Middle East, have unfortunately brought Islam into focus in discussions on terrorism. Here it must be noted that, while defending one's faith has been part of Islamic history, terrorism and suicide have no religious sanction in Islam. In fact, most moderate Muslims and interpreters of Islamic teachings would challenge the idea that these are part of the practice of Islam. Therefore, in Islamic mainline thinking there is little support for terrorism as a way of attracting attention to causes, even if they are deemed to be just. Terrorist activities, in this context, must be seen as the choice of disaffected groups who interpret and use Islamic teachings to draw inspiration and justification for their actions.

Some Christians have lifted up verses in the Quran to argue that Islam is a militaristic religion that supports terrorism, not realizing that verse for verse the Bible would come out as a religious scripture that supports violence more than any other body of scripture! We need to respect how scriptures, written in a different century in a different context, are understood in each of our religious traditions. And we should allow each community to speak for itself.

Responses to terrorism

Today there is also considerable discussion on the way terrorism is being defined and countered. Some governments have begun to identify any form of struggle or challenge to their authority as a terrorist threat; questionable laws and practices have been instituted as part of the war on terrorism. Those concerned with human rights and the rule of law have begun to question unjustified arrests and long detentions of persons from specific ethnic or religious groups as part of the anti-terrorist programme.

There is no doubt that some acts of terrorism arise from hatred and malice and should be resisted and stopped. Criminals groups involved in such acts need to be brought to justice. The 11 September attack on the Twin Towers, the train and bus bombings in Madrid and Jerusalem, the bombing of a theatre in Moscow and the gas attack on the Tokyo subway are kinds of terrorist attacks that have been roundly condemned. Here attempts are made to bring about maximum harm to civilians who have no part in the controversy.

In the context of the Middle East conflict, there is also an important issue arising from the meaning and use of the word "martyrdom". The classical understanding of a martyr is of one who is willing to lay down one's life, if necessary, instead of denying or compromising one's faith or one's cause. In fact the word "martyr" simply means a "witness" – the testimony of laying down one's life for what one believes in. Religious history is full of martyrs who readily suffered persecution and death rather than deny their faith or principles.

This word has been given a new meaning in our day. The groups that sent attackers to the Twin Towers and suicide bombers targeted on the Middle East call them "martyrs". What is more, those who do these acts also believe that they are engaging in martyrdom. The problem with the use of the word is that, as mentioned earlier, in the classical under-standing of martyrdom one gives one's life for the cause, but does not take the lives of others. Therefore, the use of the word martyrdom for actions that also kill innocent people is misleading, even though it is true that one is, in fact, laying down one's life for one's cause.

Addressing the problem

Today there is a growing conviction among many that it is not enough only to condemn these persons and try to pre-vent them from reaching their targets. While this remains necessary, attention is also being drawn to the need to deal with the fundamental issues that drive people to take their own lives and the lives of others.

For a long time it was generally believed that terrorists and suicide bombers are brain-washed in religious or ideo-logical camps and that they act out of emotional impulses, manipulated by those who train them. This analysis was based on a conviction that no one would so readily lay down his or her life unless under considerable mental and psycho-logical manipulation.

The 11 September attacks, however, has placed a big question mark against this easy assumption. Most of the attackers were well beyond teen-age years; they had under-gone a long period of training; they had taken the trouble to register as students in pilot training schools and had under-gone a training process in preparation for boarding jetliners. It is believed that those who sent them to attack the Towers were not in the country to whip up their mental and emo-tional state of readiness to give their lives. It would appear that the decision to commit suicide was not impulsive, rash or rushed. There was painstaking decision-making, training and execution. Similarly, two of the future suicide bombers interviewed by a reporter for CNN (shown on 4 April 2004) appeared calm, collected, determined and ready to die for their cause.

All this means that while governments do have the responsibility of stopping attacks on innocent civilians, they fail their own people if they, at the same time, fail to deal with the underlying causes that lead to terrorist attacks. One of the most disappointing dimensions of the news coverage in the mainstream media in the USA is that there was very little analysis of why some groups are bent on perpetrating attacks on US citizens and interests. Soon after the attacks in 2001, the administration explained simply that "they do not like our way of life", "they are against our civilization", "they are against democracy", "they attack us because we are the most powerful nation in the world" and so on. One listened to these reasons in total disbelief, but with understanding, because everyone including the country's leaders appeared to be in a state of confusion at the enormity of the event.

But a year later there was still too little analysis, but only a festering sense of grievance. Those who do engage in deeper analysis never get on prime-time television. With regard to the Israeli-Palestinian conflict in the Middle East, there is very little confidence left that the violence and counter-violence plaguing the region can any longer be addressed without resolving the underlying socio-economic-political-land issues. No nation can build a wall long and high enough to protect itself from others. While concrete walls may give temporary protection, it is clear to all that what needs to fall down is the wall of suspicion and hatred which has grown up between two peoples. Arabs and Jews have lived together in peace and harmony in this very region during many periods of history. Even today, despite all the problems, many Israelis and Palestinians believe that they can live together in peace if a just political settlement can be agreed concerning the apportioning of the land. Everyone is held hostage by the extremists on both sides.

It is important that the powerful nations come to a realization of the link between global terror and global economics. Deep economic disparities that keep peoples in abject poverty or under oppression, in any part of the world, are breeding grounds for violence. It is here that those who foment terrorism find their recruits. This has been said often

enough, but no government seems to take it with the seriousness it deserves. It is unrealistic to expect those who have
been disenfranchised of power, pushed against the wall and
left with no hope for the future, not to resort to desperate
methods to attract the attention of the world.

State terrorism

While on the subject of terrorism, it is important to draw
attention to another dimension of the issue, namely the problem of state terrorism, where the state, which is expected to
protect the people, becomes the perpetrator of violence over
sections of the population or in territories under its control.
This results in alienation and counter-violence against the
state. State terrorism in some Latin American countries has
taken the form of indiscriminate arrests, torture, summary
executions, disappearances and abductions.

In the Middle East, state terrorism includes intimidation,
mass arrests, indefinite detentions, economic blockades,
destruction of homes, collective punishments and extra-judi-
cial executions. These forms of state terrorism are prohibited
by international law and regularly condemned by the United
Nations and the International Court. But some governments
pay little heed to these international institutions and act with
impunity. It should come as no surprise that counter-terror
attacks and suicide bombings are on the increase, feeding the
cycle of violence.

The need for new thinking

Part of the discussion of violence must involve becoming
more discriminating in the reading of the Bible. The thirst for
"power" that accompanies violence has been an abiding
temptation not only to nations and empires but also to religious traditions. Christianity for its part has succumbed to
the lure of power, both in its theological expressions, ecclo-
sial structures and mission practices. Therefore, Christians
ought to engage in honest self-examination to understand
how our tradition has incorporated, consciously or unconsciously, structures of domination, power, exclusion and dis-

crimination in its teachings, practices and structures. Thanks partly to theological insights from those who "see history from the underside", the rise of feminism and some dimensions of post-modern criticism, Christianity has started to look more closely at itself in relation to religion and violence. This is no more than a tentative beginning.

The issue, however, is not peculiar to the Christian religion. Violence in society and violence in the way religion expresses itself are common problems that need to engage the attention of all religious traditions. And no religion has been free from flirting with powers-that-be for the sake of advancement. Each religious community has to examine its own life and look for ways of countering the prevalent culture of violence in so many dimensions of our life. We would live in peace, yet peace eludes us.

The greatest gift humankind has is its capacity to organize its own life, and the possibility to imagine what it might be. The culture of violence was not thrust upon us. We created it, little by little, until we became its prisoners. We can also undo this culture of violence, if only we have the will and the passion to do so. We turn to this issue in the final chapter.

7. Axis of Peace

In his book *Religion and Violence*, Robert McAfee Brown quotes a graffiti slogan written on the walls of a subway station in Paris:

Be realistic – attempt the impossible!

I am intrigued by the sentiment expressed in this phrase, for it could easily have been the title of a book on the life and teachings of Christ. In fact, much of what the gospel writers present as the teachings of Jesus – "turn the other cheek", "love your enemies", "bless them that curse you", "pray for them that persecute you", "do not repay evil for evil", "overcome evil with good" and so on – appears to indulge in idealism in the area of violence that is not appropriate for us humans! These teachings come through as naive, impractical and other-worldly. While Jesus appears to have had quite a following, his own public ministry was short-lived. In subsequent history, many others, who advocated and attempted to put these ideals into actual practice, were also cut down. The well-known in our own day include persons like Mahatma Gandhi and Martin Luther King Jr. While they are held as heroes, their passion for and advocacy of radical nonviolence were burned or buried with them.

Are we here dealing with the love-hate relationship we humans have with violence, as was mentioned earlier? There appears to be something deep within us that sees the nonviolent approach to life as the right way and something worthy of celebration. And yet, we appear to be too insecure, realistic and just plain down-to-earth to dare to believe that nonviolence can indeed be the principle on which to build our personal, communal and international lives. In fact, the church comes to our assistance on this matter in its traditional teachings. It helps us to quietly substitute "belief" in Jesus Christ for "discipleship" and teaches us to take our refuge in his cross rather than carry our own crosses in standing up to the forces of violence in our day.

People of other religious traditions would be able to tell their own stories. In almost every religion, if the founders demanded radical nonviolence, uncompromising love for one's neighbours, self-denial and renunciation of those who follow them, the institutionalized expressions of those religions manage to "tone down" these teachings to "realistic proportions". Those who inherit the founders' ministries appear to believe that to ask too much is to defeat the whole purpose! Perhaps one needs to be reduced to poverty and deprivation, powerlessness and hopelessness – to the point of having nothing else but the walls of a subway station on which to make a statement – to have the courage to say: "Be realistic – attempt the impossible!"

The debate between the idealists and realists is ongoing in the field of ethics. Some hold that ethical values have to be absolute and must be held up despite the fact that we do not always live up to them; anything else would appear to them to be a compromise. Others, while not denying the absolute nature of key values, argue that the only way to help human beings move towards those ideals is to create doable "middle axioms" that cut a pathway towards the ideal. It is not my intention here to enter this debate. What actually troubles most people today is that gradually we have not only allowed a culture of violence to seep deep into all dimensions of life, but also appear to have accepted it as inevitable. Violence is increasingly becoming the only way we seek to deal with problems in personal, societal and international relations. The question is this: Is there another way? Should we indeed "be realistic, and attempt the impossible"?

Axis of Peace

Many who were listening to President George W. Bush's state of the union address to a joint session of the US congress in January 2002 were taken aback to hear him say, as if out of the blue, that Iran, Iraq and North Korea formed an "Axis of Evil". It raised many questions. Why only these three, of all the nations of the world? What is meant by the phrase "Axis of Evil"? Is this a helpful way to deal with these nations? What tone does it set for US foreign policy? Who decides whether a particular nation is "evil", and on what basis?

During the controversy that followed Bush's speech, the best response that I came across was a proposal for an alternate Axis of Evil. I heard this in a speech by the general secretary of the National Council of the Churches of Christ in the USA, Bob Edgar, who attributed its formulation to someone else. "The only Axis of Evil we need to confront is this," he said. "Endemic poverty, devastation of the environment and the weapons of mass destruction." I felt it was a well-conceived "axis" and touched some of the real dangers that threaten the well-being of all humankind.

But as I brooded over this fine formulation it occurred to me that perhaps we should go even further in providing yet another alternative, perhaps a positive one. Hence the *Axis of Peace: Christian Faith in Times of Violence and War.*

The problem with this proposed Axis is that it states the obvious. Who can be against justice, reconciliation and non-violence? Are not all religious traditions in this business? Would not all states agree that this is what needs to be done? Indeed. And yet, I believe that these three ideas need to be revisited in our own times, especially from the angle of rampant violence that has become so much a part of our lives. And the goal, of course, is not that one would immediately find ways of implementing them or be able to eradicate violence. Rather, it is hoped that reflections on the three aspects of the Axis, especially at the congregational level, may enable us to recognize the seriousness of the issue and the need to do something about it, albeit in small measures. The Chinese philosopher Lao Tzu says, "The journey of a thousand miles must begin with a single step." The intention to raise awareness and to animate small ways of responding to the issue of violence was also one of the dimensions of the WCC programme for a Decade to Overcome Violence.

It is of interest that the focus of the programme is not to "eliminate" violence, to "crush" violence or even to "counter" violence but to "overcome" it. I was at a worship service during the meeting of the central committee of the World Council of Churches in Johannesburg, South Africa, when the first seeds of the programme were sown. The South

African bishop who preached the sermon at that service thanked the World Council of Churches for its Programme to Combat Racism that had played a significant role in supporting the struggle against the apartheid system in South Africa. The World Council, despite concerted opposition from some Christian and other groups, had maintained that racism is a sin that militates against the gospel. The programme became a concrete way of demonstrating that belief.

Now that apartheid as a system had collapsed, would the WCC turn its attention to the issue of violence? Even though South Africa, under the wise leadership of Nelson Mandela, would do everything possible to prevent a much-feared outbreak of widespread violence aimed at revenge and reprisal against the white population, violence in general was still to be a problem in South Africa. In any case, many other countries in Africa were being ripped apart by violent internal conflicts. The bishop at Johannesburg called upon the WCC to initiate a new programme – the "Programme to Combat Violence".

The intention was clear, and the call was timely. But would the word "combat" be appropriate for a programme that seeks to deal with the issue of violence? The verb we would use would indicate the realism, seriousness and spirit in which we approached the issue. The verb that finally emerged was "overcome". Some felt that the verb was rather passive and would fail to capture the sense of urgency that should inspire the programme; others claimed that even the world "overcome" had militaristic undertones, as in overcoming one's enemy in the battlefield. Yet, most people felt that it did capture the need to confront the problem of violence, and yet moved away from the more militaristic notion involved in the word "combat". I was satisfied because what was ringing in my own ears was the African American spiritual that became the theme song of the nonviolent struggle against racism and for civil rights in the United States: "Deep in my heart, I do believe; we shall *overcome* some day!"

With this background to the programme, let us turn to the first dimension of the axis: justice.

1. Justice: the condition for peace

The word "justice" has a built-in problem. Like the word love it is also one of the most used, misused and abused among words. Everyone has their own take on it; some even fear the word because they have come to associate it with some kind of "communist" ideology or "liberal" thinking! If one were to walk into a well-dressed evening party and admit that his or her job is to "work for justice in society", that person would not be surrounded by too many other people wanting to engage him or her in a lively conversation. Some fear the very word "justice".

Yet, "justice" is also much used. Every time there is an execution as the culmination of capital punishment, people appear on the TV screen and say that they feel that "justice" has been done! Brutal dictators round up persons who have advocated the rights of the people in order to "bring them to justice"! Some of the most violent and ruthless armed factions in several countries claim that they are fighting for a just cause. Then there is a whole court system to dispense "justice".

Much can be said about justice, but in the Bible the word justice is not an abstract concept; it has to do with concrete relationships. In biblical teachings the nature of the relationships that we build with each other, and the kind of social, economic and political arrangements we make to live in community would be either just or unjust. In other words, justice, in the Bible, has to do with three dimensions of what goes into the building up of personal and social relationships:
– the use, distribution and access to power that regulate relationships;
– the protection and preservation of human dignity; and
– our approach to those who have become marginalized for a number of reasons.

No doubt, much more can be said on the many facets that the word justice denotes. But our purpose here is to see the relationship between violence and justice. One could take any of the forms of violence we have discussed earlier, such as violence against women, social violence like racism or casteism, the economic violence of domination, or active violence in warfare: they would fall under one or a combination of these three dimensions of the issue. In other words, there can be no justice when power is abused, human dignity is trampled upon or provisions are not made for the socially, economically and politically disadvantaged.

With this basis, let us turn to the first of the biblical principles of justice.

Use, misuse and abuse of power in human relationships

All human relationships have an inevitable power dimension. It is foolish not to recognize and acknowledge it. As a husband, father, teacher, preacher, ecumenical worker, and as an employee of my church and my university, I am constantly, but perhaps unconsciously, dealing with power. Power itself is not bad. But since it has to be exercised to animate relationships, the question of how it is used becomes a central issue in human interactions. It is here that we see the intersection between power and justice. The exercise of power, however, regulates not only personal relationships but also the relationship between communities and nations. Unjust relations come from the abuse of power.

Just relations at the personal level

Whenever I read the Sermon of the Mount, where Matthew attempts to gather together Jesus' teachings on a variety of subjects, I am inevitably struck by the demands his teaching made on the hearers.

> You have heard that it was said to those of ancient times, "You shall not murder"; and whoever murders shall be liable to judgment. But I say to you that if you are angry with a brother or sister, you will be liable to judgment;... And if you say, "You fool", you will be liable to the hell of fire.

Again,

> You have heard that it was said, "You shall not commit adultery." But I say to you that everyone who looks at a woman with lust has already committed adultery with her in his heart. (Matt. 5:21-22,27-28)

My thought is, "Is Jesus really serious here? Surely this is to ask too much!" In fact, the gospel narrative says that at some point some of Jesus' followers left him because they found his teachings too hard to take (cf. John 6:66).

It is only over the years that I have come to have a greater understanding of what Jesus was after. Jesus refuses to deal with the *expression* of violence but with its *source*. Murder does not just happen; specific persons commit it. Not all persons commit murder, but some do. And those who commit murder don't suddenly decide to do so but have *become persons* capable of contemplating and doing it. Anger and hatred towards one's brother or sister also comes from the very same source that prompts persons to commit murder. Therefore Jesus' basic conviction is that a good tree cannot bear bad fruits, and a bad tree cannot bear good fruits: "Are grapes gathered from thorns, or figs from thistles? In the same way, every good tree bears good fruit, but the bad tree bears bad fruit" (Matt. 7:16-17).

Having been a pastor of many congregations over a period of time I came to the conclusion that there were two kinds of men in all my congregations: those who respected women and those who considered them in some sense inferior to men. This had implications for how they treated their wives at home, how they dealt with women in the committees of the church and how they treated women in their place of work. A bad tree cannot bear good fruit.

The implications of Jesus' teachings here are far-reaching. In the area of personal relationships, in the last analysis, just relations cannot be legislated, enforced or preached. They have to be cultivated. One needs to work towards a culture of mutual respect and a spirituality of relatedness as the milieu in which children grow to become responsible members of society. In other words, the values that foster just personal relations cannot be mandated; they have to be instilled.

One has to assume that one of the fundamental purposes of religious traditions is to instill these values and to create spirituality in people trusting that this will lead to just relations. For me, the most disappointing dimension of most religious traditions is not so much that they are used and abused in conflict situations, but that their self-definitions and the way they look at other religious traditions are quite contrary to the spirituality of inter-relatedness.

One of the reasons why religions get so easily co-opted in violent situations, and why religious sentiments could so easily be used to fan hatred, is the reality that they already have exclusive, intolerant and anti-relational attitudes built into their self-definitions and doctrines. Thus, while religions are in theory in favour of justice, peace and love, the doctrines and structures of most religions do not promote or nurture a spirituality of just relations across religious barriers. The search for just relations, therefore, requires a thorough rethinking on the part of religious traditions concerning the impact their teachings have on the search for a wider community that is just and peaceful.

But religion is not the only force that shapes and nurtures relationships. Today the mass media, in the form of television, radio, internet, cinema, music, novels and newspapers, nurture our spirits. In most of our countries this nurturing leaves much to be desired. A society cannot be expected to overcome violence when violence is at the heart even of the entertainment and games industry.

Some months back I was on a daytime flight between Geneva and Newark, which is about a seven-hour journey. Seated near me was a family, and one of the children, a 10-year-old boy, had with him a hand-held computer game station. For nearly five of the seven hours he was shooting down cars, planes, extra-terrestrial objects and people who appeared with their own shooting powers from all corners of the screen, thoroughly enjoying all the successes and deeply disappointed when he failed to shoot down the "enemies". As I was getting off the plane, I could not stop wondering what these five hours of his life would have instilled in him as a person and would contribute to the way he looked at the world.

What we sow is what we reap.

What the game does to the little boy is to teach him to overpower everyone who appears on his screen, and to be in "total control" of the situation. He needed to do whatever it took to assert himself as the winner. His victory was predicated on the demise of others, and each time he succeeded in overcoming his enemies, the game provided a higher level of challenge that required of him even greater determination and power.

The parallels between this approach and the reasons why people use violence in personal relations are too obvious to describe.

Just relations at the social level

The role of power in just and unjust relations is more obvious at the level of a society. There is no need here to recount or to analyze social injustices like racism, casteism, sexism, homophobia, xenophobia, suppression of ethnic, religious, indigenous minorities. The litany of the social ills that beset us is rehearsed in almost every ecumenical gathering.

From the perspective of this discussion, what is important to note is that perhaps no other social institution is more guilty of perpetrating, sustaining and justifying unjust relations at the social level than religions themselves. Most societies are built on religious visions. Even societies that are deemed to be "secular" in our day are built on religious foundations that were laid in an earlier age.

These religious visions, for the most part, are hierarchical, patriarchal and justify unjust distribution of power. Confucianism and Shinto advocate a hierarchical society as a social vision. Hinduism gives scriptural justification to the caste system. Judaism, Christianity and Islam, despite the rethinking that is in progress, are hierarchical, patriarchal in their most common expressions. Even "protest religions" like Buddhism, Sikhism and Jainism succumb to the pressure of power relations in their institutional manifestations.

It is little wonder that Jesus was at odds with religious and political elites from the very beginning of his ministry. His refusal to accommodate to the existing power relations was also to result in his rejection.

This is a difficult issue for religious traditions. Institutionalization of religions is inevitable because we human beings need to live together, and this invariably leads to the need for formal institutions. Institutions are nothing more than the organizing of power relations so that there is a basis around which the society may cohere. The common problem that one confronts here is the issue of idealism and reality. A blanket rejection of institutions, or to deny that power relations are part of all social life, would be foolhardy. Power is needed to implement things, to change things and to accomplish what needs to be done. But, at the same time, it is equally foolhardy to pretend that social institutions are innocent, that a particular model of power distribution is inevitable and that institutions cannot be remodelled to overcome the violence they embody and promote in society.

The truth of the matter is that there are very many ways to organize religious traditions and the society in general. Power can indeed be more widely distributed if there is the will. It can be exercised in different ways and one does make choices on the matter. Institutions can be restrictive or liberating, oppressive or enabling, transparent or opaque, just or unjust. Therefore, part of the search for justice in the process of overcoming violence is to be attentive to the social violence that goes with social organization, and to be ready to change as the situation demands.

There appears to be reluctance on the part of religious traditions to discuss the issue of power relations and their impact on violence. Violence is used to acquire, maintain, protect and sustain power; violence is used to challenge, rebel against and to de-legitimize power; violence is used to contain, crush or to eliminate those who challenge power. Therefore, one cannot work towards overcoming violence without paying attention to the power issue and the role and complicity of religions in this area.

It is of interest that the gospel narrative says that Jesus was "driven" by the Spirit to be tempted in the wilderness before be could begin his public ministry (Mark 1:12). All the temptations appear to relate to only one issue: the temptation to power – the power to be in control of his own affairs (to make bread out of stones), the power to impress and win people over (jump from the pinnacle of the temple) and the power of "total control" (the power of owning everything his eyes could see). It would appear that, having been baptized in the waters of Jordan, Jesus had also to go through a "baptism of fire" – the temptation to grab power, and the capacity to overcome it – in order to be worthy of the ministry entrusted to him.

Justice as the protection and preservation of human dignity

The second area of justice in the biblical message has to do with human dignity. My many years of work within the ecumenical movement have taken me to over fifty countries of the world. I have had the opportunity to interact with the Maori people in Aotearoa-New Zealand, Aboriginals in Australia, Filippino domestic workers in Hong Kong, Sri Lankan and Tibetan refugees and the Dalits ("outcasts") in India, Indian estate labourers in Sri Lanka, tribal peoples of Thailand, Palestinians in the West Bank, Muslim migrants in Germany, Native American groups in North and South America. In addition, I have also seen some of the most deplorable and heart-rending poverty in the slums of Asia and in several African countries. In pastoral settings, I have come across women and children who are abused and mistreated. All that experience has left me with one major irrevocable conviction: True religion and true justice have to do with the affirmation of each and every person's dignity. Where human dignity is trampled upon, there is no true religion. And all forms of organizing of human life – social, economic and political – that do not protect and preserve human dignity are corrupt, unjust and violent.

For all the difficulties I have with many parts of the Bible, I love the book because of its unequivocal affirmation of the dignity of the human person. The opening chapters of the Bible have the courage to declare that human beings are created in the image and likeness of God. The prophetic tradition is relentless in its demand for justice, spelled out as ensuring the basic needs of all people, and not denying justice to anyone because they are poor or find themselves at the margins of society.

When one does see the staggering inequalities in the world – the dehumanizing poverty that leads to the death of millions due to hunger and disease, the arrogance with which peoples' dignity is trampled upon in social relations, the impunity with which the politically powerful unleash violence on the powerless, the callousness with which armed forces drop bombs on civilians and cities, the unimaginable greed that governs corporate profits and the mindlessness with which the earth's resources are exploited and the earth itself is devastated for the excesses of a few – I am personally surprised that there is only so much, and not much more, violence in the world.

One could give an endless list of statistics to quantify the injustices that plague the production, distribution, and consumption of the earth's resources. One could offer chapter and verse to show how international financial and trade institutions favour the rich and the powerful nations and seek to exploit even further the poor and the disadvantaged. On these, there is much written, and the statistics can be accessed on appropriate websites.

The point is clear. Justice is an important component in the Axis of Peace. Where there is no justice, there can be no peace. The violence of injustice gives birth to violence on the part of the victimized. Violence cannot be overcome by treating the symptoms, but by curing the causes.

A good tree cannot bear bad fruit.

Justice as an approach to the disadvantaged

One of the fascinating dimensions of the Bible is its realism in recognizing that there will always be the disadvantaged and marginalized persons in any society. Therefore it does not seek to establish a classless society or even a society in which there is no one who is disadvantaged or becomes marginalized. Utopian hopes are left to eschatological visions of the perfected new heaven and new earth! In the meantime, the Bible holds, we have to deal with the disadvantaged.

This sentiment runs against much of the thinking that permeates the culture of our day. The predominant culture's view is expressed in the statement, "Each one for him- or herself; and God for us all." Those who lag behind are blamed for not having "made it", for it is generally believed that there is "equal opportunity" for all who are born in a democratic, capitalistic society. That persons may be born into poverty, into families that care little to motivate children, with mental or physical disability or that unexpected calamities could fall on them is never understood. The myth of "equal opportunity" and the sentiment that "everybody can make it if they really want to do so" blind people to the profound justice issues involved.

It is here that the Bible is revolutionary. It never blames the victims. On the contrary, it shows God on the side of the poor and the marginalized. And it makes demands on society to take responsibility for the well-being of all. Today not only people but also whole nations are marginalized. The poorer nations are simply excluded from the tables where global decisions are made. The rich nations create "clubs" among themselves to manage the economic affairs of the world. Some nations are written off and others are left to wallow in their poverty, disease and consequent internal conflicts. The richer nations use the United Nations only when necessary and simply refuse to accept treaty obligations.

The biblical insight on this is that the well-being of the whole is profoundly related to the well-being of the parts that constitute it. The rampant violence we see today, in the forms of terrorism, suicide bombings and internal conflicts, stems from causes allowed to fester at the margins.

The violence of justice denied at the margins results in counter-violence at the centre. In other words, there can be no real peace in the world until justice is done at the margins of society.

2. Reconciliation: the way to peace

Human attempts to check and deter violence

Violence, of course, is a major issue for all societies. It needs to be addressed because it disrupts and destroys life in community. Governments seek to deal with expressions of violence through different agencies like the police or the armed forces, as the situation demands. It is their duty to protect citizens and to "bring to justice" those who perpetrate violence on society. As seen earlier, most people think that a limited and judicious use of force on the part of the state to deter and contain violence is inevitable. No society has been able to organize its common life without laws of one form or another and mechanisms to deal with those who break them.

However, in all cultures there are also mechanisms to offer an opportunity for those who break the law to explain or to defend themselves. Long before the appearance of formal law courts to dispense justice, all societies appear to have had in place some mechanism for this process. In Indian villages, for instance, the offender was brought before the *panchayat,* a council of elders of the village, to listen to the aggrieved party, to give an opportunity to the offender to explain him or herself, and to pronounce what might be done in response. In the Native American tradition the offenders were brought before the chief of the tribe who sat with a council of elders to plead the case. In urban situations this principle of having to listen to all parties has been developed into a full-scale judicial system with lawyers to prosecute and to defend, with a jury, a judge or a group of judges to decide on the response that would be appropriate.

What is most interesting in the whole system, whether at the village level or in a highly developed judicial apparatus, is that there is a twofold concern in dealing with violence. On the one hand, there is recognition that when individual rights or the laws drawn up to help life in community are violated, the community should find ways to deal with it. On the other, there is a deliberate attempt to give an opportunity to the person who committed the violation to defend him- or herself.

There appear to be three emphases to this second aspect of the judicial system. The first is to establish through recognized processes that the person in fact committed the act of violence for which he or she is accused. The second, equally important, is to determine the circumstances and the reasons why violation took place. This is important because the violation may have happened by accident, in self-defence, out of desperation, when the person was not in control of him- or herself, when he or she did not have the mental or psychological capacity to know the consequences of the action. It is interesting that in most situations the judicial system is weighted on the side of the accused, and the burden is placed on the prosecutors to "prove beyond reasonable doubt" that the violation took place and that the person concerned should be held "responsible" for his or her actions. The third aspect, when one is found guilty, is to ensure that the punishment given is in proportion to the violation, and where possible, is directed towards restoration for the victim and the rehabilitation of the culpable person.

Unfortunately this elaborate system, carefully developed and fine-tuned through many schools of jurisprudence, deals with maintaining justice within given societies. What of the relationship between nations? There are indeed international laws on matters concerning which nations are willing to subject themselves to laws, in their own self-interest and in the interest of all. Shipping in the open seas, air traffic across national boundaries, the use of outer space, and so forth, are examples of subjects on which it is in the interest of all nations to develop commonly acknowledged procedures. Like the courts of law in nations, there is also an international court to pass judgment on international disputes. And anything not covered by international law is dealt with through commonly negotiated agreements, covenants, treaties and conventions. The United Nations Organization plays the key role in bringing nations together, in providing the forum for discussion and drawing up agreements.

Regrettably, none of these are binding on nations, for there is no real external authority that has been given power over all the nations to enforce these laws and agreements. The UN represents a forum, and while it can enforce decisions under some circumstances, it is not a final instrument of global governance. Not all countries enter international agreements; some flout them systematically with impunity; and some of the powerful nations simply ignore or break them at will.

The point of this discussion is to show that humankind has, in fact, taken pains to organize its life on the basis of what is fair and just. It has also developed mechanisms to prevent, contain and, where necessary, administer justice when these arrangements are breached. And yet violence within and between nations is raging as an uncontrollable fire. Did we get it all wrong? Is there another way to go?

The enormity of the issue

The enormity of the issue, and the limitations of the entire systems of national and international laws and their applications came home to me when I visited South Africa some time after the dismantling of the apartheid system. A minority of whites had been ruling ruthlessly over the majority black population, brutally dealing with any form of dissent. The minority rule was based on a dehumanizing ideology that introduced inferiority and superiority on the basis of the colour of one's skin, and a vicious police force to enforce it.

Now the tables had been turned. The black people had come to power. What of the injustices of the past? How does one bring a whole system to justice? How does one build a nation out of two communities that, in the old system, were socially and legally deemed mutually exclusive?

The genius of the political and religious leadership of South Africa was to turn to the concept of "reconciliation". It is not my intention to deal here with the work of the Truth and Reconciliation Commission that helped the nation to recover its soul and to move away from the brink of disaster. But we need to look more closely at the meaning and application of the concept of reconciliation, which is proposed as a component of the Axis of Peace.

The second time I went to South Africa, this time to Cape Town, I went on a "pilgrimage" to Robben Island where Nelson Mandela had spent most of his 27 years of imprisonment. I called it a pilgrimage because I felt that it was the island where a spirituality was developed that prevented South Africa from an impending disaster.

Mandela came to the World Council of Churches soon after his release from prison. Most of those who gathered to listen to him expected him to dwell on the atrocities of apartheid rule, the greatness of the struggle against it, the sacrifices that had been made and certainly of the hardships of 27 years of life in high security prisons.

Not a word on any of these. "I have come to you to thank you", he said, "for your solidarity with us meant so much to us in the years of struggle." The rest of his speech was on the need to build a multiracial South Africa on the foundations of justice, reconciliation and peace, so that what had happened in South Africa would never happen again, there or anywhere else.

I sat there listening to him in total disbelief. How could this man, whose whole youth had been robbed of him, who was the victim of one of the worst forms of discrimination and who now had the power to move a whole nation to "pay" for what had been done to him and to his people, stand up there and say nothing – yes, nothing – that his audience expected him to say! Not a trace of resentment, no anger and no desire to avenge, even to keep the negative memories alive.

Wisdom came from Robben Island! And hence my "pilgrimage".

Reconciliation: the way to peace

When it comes to dealing with the larger issues of violence committed upon one community by another, different peoples have responded differently. In Sri Lanka, the two communities in conflict have lived in peace for centuries. And an overwhelming majority of them still do. However, the historical memories of the wars between the kings of the majority Sinhalese and minority Tamil communities is kept alive in myths that caricature and blame each other; some of these myths even get printed in school textbooks. In the former Yugoslavia, it would appear that the historical animosity between the different groups is remembered and handed down from generation to generation.

The traumatic experience of the *shoah* or the holocaust has left a very deep impression on the Jewish psyche, and there is no agreement within the Jewish community on what to do with that experience. Many firmly believe that they should never let the Jewish people or the world forget what happened, so that it will never happen again. Therefore sections of the Jewish community expend significant resources and energy in building holocaust memorials and setting up departments of holocaust studies in universities. Others fear the long-term impact of perpetuating a victim mentality on the community and see no wisdom in making such a traumatic event the organizing principle of the Jewish community's relationship to the world. As a person from outside the community, I recall having the same ambivalent feeling as I walked out of the holocaust museum in Israel.

It is difficult to pass judgments or give advice from outside to any community that has undergone suffering. Each chooses its own response. But what is important to note is that all the groups given as examples here, and many other such groups around the world, appear never to have resolved the problems that beset them if they keep only the negative memories alive. In fact, in places like Sri Lanka, Bosnia and Northern Ireland, these unhealed memories plague subsequent generations and throw them into new cycles of violence.

The biblical word for healing memories and breaking the cycle of violence is "reconciliation". The greatest benefit reconciliation provides is that it opens the possibility of creating new memories. But the problem with reconciliation is that it is a difficult option. Innocent, attractive and simple as it sounds, in reality it takes enormous spiritual stamina and courage for a person or a community to opt for reconciliation as the way forward.

Some people reject the idea of reconciliation because they are not prepared to meet the demands it would make. Others reject it because they misunderstand it and think that it's a call to "forgive and forget", to "kiss and make up"! In fact, reconciliation is a difficult *process* and has many elements to it. It is of interest to note that the South African commission appointed to deal with the past and to rebuild the relationship between blacks and whites was not instituted as a commission on "reconciliation" but on "*truth* and reconciliation". The "truth" is the painful part of it all.

Those who have worked on these questions identify several elements in the process of reconciliation.

First, there needs to be a *recognition and willingness to admit* that what has gone wrong cannot be fixed by further use of violence or by the efforts of only one of the parties involved. To most communities this realization comes too late. A WCC pastoral team sent to Sri Lanka after the first major inter-ethnic riots, as far back as 1958, already made the judgment that Sri Lanka suffered the familiar problem in conflict resolutions of "too little, too late". While the problems could still be resolved by some concessions being made on the part of both parties, there would be groups within either or both communities that would think that, with a little bit more of a show of force, they might yet be able to resolve the problem without having to give any concessions at all! At that time, the majority Sinhalese government had to negotiate a settlement with only one major political group representing the Tamil side, which was attempting to reach a settlement through nonviolent struggle.

Twenty years later, the Tamil claim had escalated from a demand for a federal constitution for the whole country to regional autonomy. There was no longer only one group to negotiate with; more groups had multiplied within the Tamil struggle, questioning the effectiveness of nonviolent and political means of seeking resolutions to the problems.

Forty years later, we have a full-fledged armed struggle between the two sides; the Tamil demand having been upgraded to nothing less than a separate Tamil State for the

Tamil people, something that is unthinkable for the Sinhalese majority.

The issue here is not about the rightness or wrongness of the Tamil demands. That discussion is beyond our scope. But after tens of thousands have died and hundreds of thousand have become refugees, still the problem can be resolved only through a negotiated settlement. But a resolution by peaceful means cannot be achieved unless both parties agree that the matter will never be resolved by violence.

We see the same situation in the Palestinian-Israeli conflict. The belief that the problem can be resolved through violence and the use of force is plunging these two peoples into unimaginable depths of violence and hatred. While the two communities kill each other, the rest of the world looks on in disbelief!

Reconciliation demands that the parties to a conflict recognize that violence or war cannot produce the answer and that they become willing to risk a more humane solution. The violent and military types within the respective communities never opt for this approach. The burden of pressuring the parties to seek reconciliation, therefore, falls on the communities themselves and on wiser leaders within the civil society. Most often they speak too little, and much too late.

The second dimension of reconciliation is *repentance*. People in general fear this word and see no social or political application for it, because the term has become so closely associated with its popular, Western, individualistically religious meaning. When the word repentance is mentioned, the image that one often conjures up is that of someone in tears at a revival meeting, deeply sorry for one's sins, falling on one's knees, asking God to accept him or her in God's loving mercy and forgiveness. There is, of course, a place in religious life for such repentance for those who need it.

However, the biblical meaning of the word is richer and has several dimensions to it. For one thing, the Greek word for repentance has more to do with the mind and will than with the heart, although the latter is not excluded. Literally it means the turning around of the mind. Repentance, in the first instance, has to do with a clear recognition and admission on the part of someone that he or she has been wrong on a matter, and that continuing to follow the course one had been following would be counter-productive. This may involve remorse, but remorse is derivative of repentance and not the thing itself. This point should be insisted upon because in social and political contexts remorse in itself has little value. Genuine repentance involves not only remorse over the path followed, but also willingness to walk a different path. Depending on the circumstances, true repentance also includes willingness to make amends for the wrong done. Repentance is the only sure sign that parties in conflict can give each other to assure themselves that there is genuine openness on all sides to create new history.

The third aspect of reconciliation is another much misunderstood word, *forgiveness*. Most of the reservations concerning this word, especially as it is applied to relationships among large communities and nations, come once again from the abuse of the word in some religious circles. Often forgiveness is presented as someone's willingness to overlook or downplay wrongs that have been done, or an act of generosity on the part of someone in power over others. In reality, the word forgiveness has to do with one of the many possible options for correcting wrongs that have been done.

The problem with the wrongs that have been done in the past is that there is no way for us to get back into the past and undo them. Therefore we have to deal with them. One way to deal with them, of course, is for the aggrieved parties to "pay back" in the same coin when they acquire the power to do so. While such "reprisals" may be claimed by the aggrieved to be morally justified, the difficulty is that retribution does not solve the problem. In fact, introducing a cycle of violence that cannot be broken will intensify the problem.

The "repentance-forgiveness" approach to the concept of reconciliation places the burden on both parties to break the cycle in order to create a new space for relationships. The offender's repentance would fall on dry ground if there were no forgiveness on the part of the victim. The victim's willingness to forgive would have no meaning unless there were repentance on the part of the offender. Both are needed in order to begin a new relationship.

What is more significant for me about forgiveness is that it not only frees the offender but perhaps more importantly it frees the victim from having to remember and nurse grievances.

In one of my confirmation classes, a student asked me whether it is "just" for God to keep forgiving sins. "I don't know about the justice part of it," I responded. "But if I were God, I would do the same thing. Imagine what a misery my life would be if I had to remember and keep account of all the sins that people are committing against me!" Everyone laughed in sympathetic agreement, and it gave us the chance to reflect on the healing and freedom we ourselves receive through our acts of forgiveness. Those who cannot forgive become prisoners of other peoples' sins.

The fundamental question we face regarding violence between communities is this: Do we want to allow the wounds to fester, or to heal?

The last dimension of the process is *reconciliation* itself. The Latin root from which the word comes means walking or coming together. Therefore in a real sense, reconciliation is not just an act, but also the beginning of "walking together" on a new road. This aspect of the meaning of reconciliation can never be over-emphasized, because if reconciliation is merely a symbolic act or a one-time gesture, there is no reason why the communities concerned would not fall apart in a matter of time. Walking together is a way to stabilize the new relationship. In order to overcome the past, we need to create a common future. We need to put in place ways of dealing with new misunderstandings, of anticipating problems and dealing with them before they overtake us. Reconciliation is thus both the culmination and the beginning of a process.

Can this principle be applied in the search for peace?

Many people tend to look upon the concept of reconciliation as more appropriate in personal disputes between indi-

viduals. Others look at the whole concept as religiously motivated and based on a rather naive approach to the problems
of the world. "We are dealing with superpowers, with nuclear
bombs, cruise missiles and military industrial complexes",
they would say. "Economic interests and political power
struggles are too complex to be addressed as problems to be
solved through reconciliation." This reservation should be
taken seriously. There is everything to be said for being honest and asking the difficult questions.

This reservation, however, arises from a caricatured
understanding of reconciliation as a pious exercise. The original meaning of reconciliation as "walking together" has
been, in popular use, enriched and extended to mean "getting
things right" or "putting things into order", as we do when
we seek to "reconcile" our bank statements. If there are dis-
crepancies in the accounts, we need to figure out what is
wrong and put things back in order. What was significant
about the work of the Truth and Reconciliation Commission
in South Africa was the courage the nation displayed in
putting the concept to the test in what appeared to be an
intractable social context of racial division.

It is no secret that not everyone was happy with the setting up of this commission, or with the bases on which it
worked. Some felt that a liberated South Africa should simply put on trial those who supported and maintained the
apartheid system and those who committed atrocities as part
of the policy of systematic oppression. Quite a few felt that
those who committed wrong were literally being allowed to
get away with murder, and that some of the confessions,
admissions and disclosures were more strategic than sincere.
Some felt that the victims and their next of kin were not
really receiving the justice they deserved. All these reservations were quite understandable. They reflected the pain and
anguish that the system had perpetrated on the people.

What is important about the commission is that it was not
set up by some "goody, goody" people who had a sentimen-
tal approach to resolving crimes of grave magnitude. Rather,
it was set up by the state through its legislature. And the com-

mission was not only a place to shed tears, but also a judicial body with the mandate of bringing people to justice. In one sense, it was a court of law.

At the same time, persons like Archbishop Desmond Tutu bore courageous witness to the power of truth, repentance, forgiveness and acceptance as values that are as relevant to social and political issues as they are in personal lives. Healing and reconciliation was the only way forward; the alternatives were unimaginable. At the same time, the process had to be as just, truthful and legal as it could be.

In all its strengths and weaknesses what the South African experiment showed was that it is indeed possible to build *processes* and *institutions* that can take deeply divisive social and political situations and deal with them in ways that break the cycle of violence and build a common future. The commission and its work under the archbishop presented a challenge to the cynicism that so pervades our culture. It was a challenge to those who thought that there was no other way than the use of power and violence to resolve social issues. It proved that what is deemed to be inevitable can indeed be changed through wise and compassionate leadership. It needed courage, faith and hope, and a stubborn confidence that we human beings can indeed rise above ourselves, to reach for something higher and more profound than what our base instincts dictate.

Here at last was a nation that was realistic enough to try the impossible, and succeed in it.

We should refuse to accept that we as human communities are not capable of building a just and peaceful world. We can. And at the heart of the Axis of Peace lies our readiness to believe that reconciliation is both desirable and possible at all levels.

3. Nonviolence: the hope for peace

Perhaps the most controversial dimension of the Axis of Peace is nonviolence. In the earlier chapters I have made statements on the issues of violence and nonviolence that are rather ambiguous. Can wars be completely avoided?

Perhaps the answer is "no"; when a country is under attack, it is unlikely that all its people will choose to remain pacifists; many would want to defend their nation and their loved ones by force of arms. Today many believe that the United Nations should have made an armed "humanitarian intervention" in Rwanda to prevent some members of the majority Hutu community from slaughtering the Tutsi minority. Eight Hundred Thousand lives were lost. We have also spoken of the need on the part of the state to use limited violence to curb widespread violence in society. In addition, there is much hesitation about criticizing an oppressed community for using violence as the last resort to free themselves.

Does this mean that we agree that violence is just and acceptable in some circumstances? My own answer is a clear "No". There are no circumstances under which violence is justified. Nonviolence is the only option open to us as intelligent beings endowed with the Spirit of God. If we are forced to bear arms to defend the nation, or to make an armed intervention to prevent a massacre, we may well end up doing so, but even those reasons do not "justify" the use of violence. If ever we have to use violence, we must do so knowing that we have been forced into choosing something that is both unacceptable and wrong.

Are we here playing with words? Are we trying both to have the cake and eat it? By no means! What is implied in the answer is that total nonviolence is the *only* true option open for us in our day. Once we believe in "reasonable" use of violence and justify its use for *any* reason, we have begun to walk the slippery slope, and it leads downhill all the way.

A careful study of the violence used in liberation struggles shows the dangers involved here. Violence has its own logic. Once it is justified and chosen as a method, it is difficult to set its limits. The intensity of the violence used is often dictated by the violence from the other side. Soon it would become necessary to use violence within the internal organization of the movement to purge it of persons who betray the cause or think differently. The use of violence changes the character of persons and organizations that use it. Violence is like cancer. It eats away from within, silently.

When we decide to use violence to prevent massacres, we are being forced to use one wrong to correct another wrong. We should never have waited until relationships between communities deteriorated to the point of using wrong instruments to do the right thing. So it is with "limited use" of violence to deter a greater violence in society or to punish those who violate laws.

Some acts of counter-violence may be necessary, but none of it is justified.

The hollowness of the principle of just use of violence becomes clear when it is applied to warfare. Once warfare is accepted as a necessity, even as the last resort, logic requires that we produce armaments, in great quantities, with great sophistication and with maximum capacity to afflict the "enemy" so that the "just war" can be won! Warfare also has its own unstoppable logic. Violence breeds and feeds on violence.

I am struck by Jesus' unequivocal firmness on the issue of violence. "Do not repay evil for evil; overcome evil with good."

Overcoming violence, therefore, involves overcoming the need to justify violence for any reason.

The road to nonviolence

The biggest drawback in the discussion on nonviolence is that often it is discussed as a theoretical concept or an ideology to which one may subscribe. Soon theoretical situations are advanced, as I have done in the opening paragraphs of this discussion, to argue that nonviolence is overly idealistic and is not viable as a position that communities and nations should adopt.

In fact, it may be counter-productive to accept nonviolence as a theoretical concept or an ideology, for soon we may find out that we are not able to live by it. My own conviction is that we should accept nonviolence not so much as an ideology to follow but as the only credible, wise and effective option open to us in dealing with human relationships. And then we may ask this question: "If we do not want to use violence to resolve issues, what alternative must we put in place to resolve them?"

We resort to violence to resolve issues because it is an easy and cowardly option. We need only our base instincts to use violence. It is not an intelligent, wise or effective way of approaching a problem. Little wonder, then, that problems are not solved and often are made even more intractable. But we humans have great powers of ingenuity, imagination and inventiveness. If violence were not available to us as a tool, we would indeed invent other tools to deal with our problems. In other words, eliminating violence as an option, under any circumstance, is the only incentive that would ensure our choice of other options.

Today, peace studies, peace education, nonviolent ways of resolving conflicts, conflict resolution and reconciliation are disciplines concerning which considerable research and training is being carried out, for increasing numbers of people have become deeply concerned with the rampant violence that has engulfed all our societies. The shameful escalation of violence in the Middle East, ever increasing internal conflicts in African and Asian countries, the rise of extremism in many religious traditions, global networks of terrorism, the mindless invasion of Iraq and its violent aftermath, unconscionable exploitation of the earth, the untenable poverty and depravation of millions of people, rampant violence in personal relationships – all this has begun to shake the consciences of people. "Surely," they say, "there must be another way."

Indeed! Violence and wars can be anticipated; they can be prevented. The reasons for violence and war can be identified; steps can be taken to remedy them. Conflicts that inevitably arise between individuals and groups can be acknowledged; nonviolent ways of resolving them can be instituted and even mandated. We can build institutions to promote reconciliation and to help people better understand the benefits of just peace. We can develop further international instruments to mediate between nations. We can even outlaw war! We can do all this if we have the collective will to do so. It is not true that things can never be different.

Such revolutionary changes cannot be brought about by governments, which work on the logic of power. Change must be implemented by the people. Not overnight, but through many small steps taken to overcome violence in its manifold forms and by affirming peace as both the way and the goal. In other words, we need to transform the culture of violence into a culture of peace and nonviolence.

Justice, reconciliation and nonviolence are presented here as coordinates of the Axis of Peace because peace cannot be achieved by emphasizing any one of them alone; they belong together. Justice is the condition required for peace to emerge; there can be no peace without justice. Reconciliation is the way to peace, because peace requires healing, both now and in our ongoing journey. And choosing nonviolence is ultimately the only way to give peace a chance.

In this way, we may also acquire the chance to prove that even this tragically fractured humankind may finally get it right.

You may ask, "All this looks good; but can justice, reconciliation and peace through nonviolence be achieved by us, ordinary people like you and me?"

I can only refer you to the grafitti on that wall in a subway station in Paris:

Be realistic – attempt the impossible!